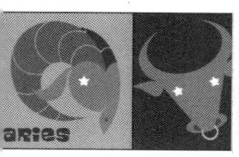

seventeen
Total Astrology

What the Stars Say about Life and Love

By Georgia Routsis Savas

A PARACHUTE PRESS BOOK

HarperCollins*Publishers*

Created and produced by
PARACHUTE PUBLISHING, L.L.C.
156 Fifth Avenue, Suite 302
New York, NY 10010

Published by
HarperCollins*Publishers*
1350 Avenue of the Americas
New York, NY 10019

Copyright © 2000 PRIMEDIA Magazines Inc., publisher of **seventeen**.
Seventeen is a registered trademark of PRIMEDIA Magazines Finance Inc.

All rights reserved. No part of this book may be used or reproduced in any manner whatsoever without written permission except in the case of brief quotations embodied in critical articles or reviews.

For information write:
Editorial Manager
seventeen
850 Third Avenue
New York, NY 10022

Design by Aleta Fedoruk/Fedoruk Designs
Cover illustration by Kirsten Ulve
Printed in Baltimore, Maryland by John D. Lucas Printing

Library of Congress Catalog Card Number: 00-104539

ISBN: 0-06-440872-8

HarperCollins® and ⛉® are trademarks
of HarperCollins Publishers Inc.

10 9 8 7 6 5 4 3 2 1

First edition, October 2000

Table of Contents

1 INTRODUCTION:
Astrology 101

10 CHAPTER ONE:
Aries (March 21 to April 19)

18 CHAPTER TWO:
Taurus (April 20 to May 20)

26 CHAPTER THREE:
Gemini (May 21 to June 20)

34 CHAPTER FOUR:
Cancer (June 21 to July 22)

42 CHAPTER FIVE:
Leo (July 23 to August 22)

50 CHAPTER SIX:
Virgo (August 23 to September 22)

58 CHAPTER SEVEN:
Libra (September 23 to October 22)

66 CHAPTER EIGHT:
Scorpio (October 23 to November 21)

74 CHAPTER NINE:
Sagittarius (November 22 to December 21)

82 CHAPTER TEN:
Capricorn (December 22 to January 19)

90 CHAPTER ELEVEN:
Aquarius (January 20 to February 18)

98 CHAPTER TWELVE:
Pisces (February 19 to March 20)

106 CHAPTER THIRTEEN:
Beyond Your Sun Sign

Acknowledgements

I would like to thank **seventeen** magazine, Parachute Publishing, and HarperCollins Publishers for giving me the opportunity to channel my celestial thoughts into book form; my editor, Ruth Ashby, for all her guidance; my personal Karmic agent, Wendy Wax, for setting me up on the blind date with **seventeen;** Ester Malatesta, for her unending knowledge of celeb birthdays and for acting as my zodiacal sounding board; my canine daughter Savannah, for forcing me out of the house for that all-important beach walk; and my ever-patient husband, Damon, for keeping my world spinning as I was chained to my Macintosh. And thanks to my family, friends, and those strangers on the street who've had to endure years of hearing me ask the same old question: *When's your birthday?*

Astrology 101 — Introduction

Do either of these scenes sound familiar?

You're fast asleep when—Buzzz!—the alarm goes off. You hit the snooze button a couple of times—and when you finally stumble out of bed, you're already fifteen minutes behind schedule. Your favorite sweater is dirty, you can't find your science homework, someone ate the last of the Frosted Mini-Flakes, and your hair looks like something nested in it. To top it all off—you miss the bus.

Maybe you should just go back to bed and start over.

You've finally met the guy of your dreams. Just looking at him in history class gives you the chills. When you discover you're both into Matchbox Twenty and Cool Ranch Doritos, you're ready to swoon. And then he asks you out. You have the coolest time you've had since you went to Disney World with your best friend in sixth grade.

Is this the relationship you've been waiting for? Or will it start out hot and heavy—and fizzle out?

Ever wonder why some days are so terrif and some are so hopeless? Why you're instantly compatible with one guy—and can't get through a conversation with another? Why some things just seem meant to be—and some don't?

Astrology might have some of the answers.

Why astrology?

Astrology can help you figure out who you are—and who you can be. It's as simple as that. It helps to answer the question **why?** Like why you always have to be in charge (or prefer to have someone else running the show). Or why you dye your hair a different color every month (or keep it the same old brown). Or why you just *have* to watch a movie from start to finish (or turn it off as soon as it starts getting boring).

Astrology has been around for over five thousand years (5,000!), making it the oldest science in the world. (It used to be called a science because it is based on observation of the natural world.)

And astrology is still popular today. There's a good reason for that: **It works.** When ancient stargazers observed the movement of the heavens, they noticed a connection between Earth and the stars and planets. They saw how the phases of the Moon affected the water's ebb and flow. How times of plenty and periods of famine coincided with the position of the stars. They noticed that certain plants grew better at different times and recognized that women's menstrual cycles seemed to follow the Moon's rhythms.

When these early astronomers realized that the sky reflected events that were happening on planet Earth, they called their newfound science **astrology**. "Astro" comes from the ancient Greek word for "star," and "logy" comes from the ancient Greek word that means "word." **So astrology is a collection of words—a philosophy—of the stars.**

No one is saying stars actually *cause* things to happen on Earth. Of course they don't. But astrologers believe that certain energies exist in the universe at any particular time. These energies are revealed in the heavens—and they affect everything that happens on Earth.

Early stargazers devised a complicated mathematical system for casting horoscopes. Today, your horoscope—or natal (birth) chart—is like a photograph of the stars from the Earth's perspective at the moment of your birth. It's kind of like a personal owner's manual that applies only to you. This natal chart provides the **key to figuring out what makes you tick**. It's based on three bits of information—your date of birth, your time of birth, and your place of birth. Nobody's got a chart that's exactly like yours—because no one else was born at exactly the same time and in exactly the same place as you were!

Astrology is based on the relationships between the Sun, the Moon, the planets (the Earth isn't included), and the twelve signs of the Zodiac. The Zodiac is the path of the stars around the heavens as seen from Earth. It is divided into twelve constellations. Approximately every thirty days, the Sun seems to move from the area of one constellation into another. This is why each of the constellations is called a **Sun sign**.

Each sign and planet has its own symbol—or glyph—so that an astrologer doesn't have to spell out everything in words. It's sort of like a universal language that can be understood around the globe. Besides looking *totally* cool.

Scope out the astro-glyphs shown in the chart below.

Planet and Sun Sign Symbols

Planet		Sign	
Sun	☉	Aries	♈
Moon	☾	Taurus	♉
Mercury	☿	Gemini	♊
Venus	♀	Cancer	♋
Mars	♂	Leo	♌
Jupiter	♃	Virgo	♍
Saturn	♄	Libra	♎
Uranus	♅	Scorpio	♏
Neptune	♆	Sagittarius	♐
Pluto	♇	Capricorn	♑
		Aquarius	♒
		Pisces	♓

Here Comes the Sun

Most astrologers agree that the Sun is the single most important part of a horoscope, which is why most astrology books and horoscope columns deal with Sun signs. The reason they chose the Sun is simple: **It is the most powerful force in the solar system.** Your Sun sign tells the story of who you are and what you're willing to do to get what you desire.

Approximate Sun Sign Dates

Aries	(March 21 to April 19)
Taurus	(April 20 to May 20)
Gemini	(May 21 to June 20)
Cancer	(June 21 to July 22)
Leo	(July 23 to Aug. 22)
Virgo	(Aug. 23 to Sept. 22)
Libra	(Sept. 23 to Oct. 22)
Scorpio	(Oct. 23 to Nov. 21)
Sagittarius	(Nov. 22 to Dec. 21)
Capricorn	(Dec. 22 to Jan. 19)
Aquarius	(Jan. 20 to Feb. 18)
Pisces	(Feb. 19 to March 20)

You may wonder whether the Sun sign dates are accurate—whether Capricorn, the Goat, for instance, is always overhead during late December and early January. Well, not really. Back when astrology was a new science, you could look up in the sky on a certain date and see the stars in exactly the position they were supposed to be. But now, a few thousand years later, the stars don't line up that neatly anymore, due to the Earth's peculiar spinning motion. So once upon a time, Capricorn was directly overhead in the sky during Christmas, but it's now in a different part of the sky. What a difference a millennium (or two) makes.

Figuring out your Sun sign's a cinch, *except* if you're born on the first or final day of a sign. Sometimes people call that **being born on the cusp.** You see, since the Sun doesn't enter and leave a sign on the exact same date every year (again, due to the wobbly spin of the Earth), someone born on March 20, 1983, has a Pisces Sun. But if you're born on that same date one year later, you're an Aries.

Note: **There's really no such thing as being born on a cusp.** Your Sun sign is either Pisces or Aries—it can't be both. So, if you're born within a day or two of the date the Sun switches from one sign or the other, you owe it to yourself to find out the real deal. Find an astrologer (or go to an astrology website) asap!

More About Sun Signs

Lots of things can be ruled by a Sun sign. When astrologers were first developing their science, they assigned different metals, plants, flowers, spices, gemstones, and colors to each of the signs. For instance, the colors for Leo are gold and orange. If you're a Leo, that doesn't necessarily mean that gold and orange are the colors that look best on you. Or that you should redecorate your room. But it does mean you might really like gold and orange—and that you feel luckier when you're wearing bright colors.

See how much your Sun sign can teach you about yourself? And there's more. Each of the twelve astrology signs falls into different groups, too. These particular groups are classified by **energy**, **quality**, and **element**.

What's Your Energy?

Each sign has either a **Yin (female)** or **Yang (male)** energy. Yin is called the **female, passive, or indirect force** because people born in a Yin sign tend to wait for things to come to them. They know how to attract energy without exerting it. Yinnies are usually introverted and see things subjectively.

Yang is considered **male, active, or direct** because people born under a Yang sign tend to go out and get whatever it is they crave, no matter what. Yangers are extroverted and objective.

Don't freak if you're female and you've got "masculine" energy (or vice versa). All Aries have Yang energy, after all—and half of them are male and half are female. **Both Yin and Yang energies are necessary in the world**, and one is not better or stronger than the other.

Astro Signs and their Energies

	Yin (Feminine)	Yang (Masculine)
Aries		☯
Taurus	☯	
Gemini		☯
Cancer	☯	
Leo		☯
Virgo	☯	
Libra		☯
Scorpio	☯	
Sagittarius		☯
Capricorn	☯	
Aquarius		☯
Pisces	☯	

What's Your Quality?

The qualities—**Cardinal, Fixed, and Mutable**—describe different ways of handling life. They reflect the changing seasons, from spring through winter. Each season begins with a new, bursting-with-energy **Cardinal** sign. The **Fixed** signs come in the middle of each season (which is just where they like to be—right in the center of things.) And the **Mutables** occur at the end, because they can't wait for the season to change and start anew. In other words, Cardinals start things up, Fixed folks keep things running, and Mutables make any changes that need to be made.

Cardinals are listed first because they're the bossiest and most independent of the bunch. They like to make it all happen. Innovations are what thrill in-charge Cardinals, but they often fizzle out after phase one.

Fixed folks are big-time stubborn. These people keep the ball rolling with their persistence and reliability long after Cardinals have become completely bored with a project. You can count on Fixed folks to get the job done.

Mutable signs hold it all together by being adaptable and flexible. They can see both sides of the picture and know what adjustments need to be made. Mutables are the glue-sticks of the bunch.

Astro Signs and their Qualities

	Cardinal	**Fixed**	**Mutable**
Aries	★		
Taurus		★	
Gemini			★
Cancer	★		
Leo		★	

Astro Signs and their Qualities (continued)

	Cardinal	Fixed	Mutable
Virgo			★
Libra	★		
Scorpio		★	
Sagittarius			★
Capricorn	★		
Aquarius		★	
Pisces			★

What's Your Element?

The four elements—**Fire, Earth, Air,** and **Water**—describe the character, or personality, of each sign. If you're a **Fire sign** (Aries, Leo, and Sagittarius), you've got courage and energy to burn. Thrill-seeking to the core, you live for passion and excitement. There's never a dull moment around Fire signs.

Earth signs (Taurus, Virgo, and Capricorn) are practical and full of common sense. Sure, they know how to have fun, but only after their homework is done. **Air signs** (Gemini, Libra, and Aquarius) like to communicate and interact socially. Conversation comes naturally to these thinkers—just ask their teachers!

More than other human beings, **Water signs** (Cancer, Scorpio, and Pisces) are led by their hearts instead of their heads. These intuitive souls think with their feelings. They are extra-sensitive, as their friends always learn.

Astro Signs and their Elements

	Fire	Earth	Air	Water
Aries	🔥			
Taurus		🌍		
Gemini			☁️	
Cancer				🌊
Leo	🔥			
Virgo		🌍		
Libra			☁️	
Scorpio				🌊
Sagittarius	🔥			
Capricorn		🌍		
Aquarius			☁️	
Pisces				🌊

So are you ready to learn all about your Sun sign? In Chapters 1 through 12, you'll find out lots about the sign you were born under—and the signs of your friends and family, too.

Aries

Chapter One

(March 21 to April 19)

Symbol:	The Ram (Butting through, please!)
Element:	Fire
Quality:	Cardinal (I'll show you who's the boss)
Energy:	Masculine/Yang
Ruler:	Mars (The macho, super-hero planet)
Color:	Fire-engine red
Gem:	Diamond
Keywords:	Pioneering, courageous, freedom-loving
Flower:	Honeysuckle, thistle

Celebrity Rams: Marlon Brando, Claire Danes, Leonardo da Vinci, Celine Dion, Aretha Franklin, Sarah Michelle Gellar, Al Gore, Melissa Joan Hart, Elton John, Ashley Judd, Eddie Murphy, Rosie O'Donnell, Sarah Jessica Parker, Diana Ross, Gloria Steinem, Vincent van Gogh, Reese Witherspoon

Here Comes the Sun

 It's no coincidence that Aries is the first sign of the Zodiac. If you're born under the sign of the Ram, **you love being Number One.** Chances are, when a trendy CD hits the music stores, you've heard about it way before everyone else (and probably saw the group in concert before they were even famous). If there's a hot new fashion accessory, you're into it before Madonna. (Well, maybe at the same time.) **Fashion Forward is your middle name.**

Since you're fueled by fire, you've got energy to burn. If it were up to you, life would be one long adventure-filled party (provided you could sleep late into the following day). You're courageous and impulsive, energetic, and always on the go. Some of the things you live for (besides parties) include video games, competitive sports, and anything that involves speed.

Being the first Cardinal sign means (let's face it) **you're bossy.** You like being in charge, and you're usually pretty good at handling the job. One of your many special talents is helping other people achieve their goals. You're always looking for the best in others. Unfortunately, your natural optimism can backfire, because you're not always the best judge of character. Rather than seeing people for what they are, you sometimes

Ram Likes:
- Being in charge
- Standing out in a crowd
- Defying authority
- Adventure
- People who take you up on a dare

Ram Dislikes:
- Losing
- Being ignored
- Fraidy cats
- Being told "no"
- Waiting

get caught up with what you (sigh) *wish* they were.

Even though on the outside Rams project superconfidence, on the inside they're just as insecure as anyone else. The difference is, the Ram understands that **everyone wears a mask**. And you've figured out if you keep up the tough-girl image long enough, what starts out as an act often turns into reality.

Aries in Love

Flirting must have been invented by an Aries. Nothing excites you more than the game of love. You've got it down to an art and never tire of the thrill of the chase. When an Aries goes out to hunt, you won't give up until your prey is caught.

The problem is, once the game is over, Rams often lose interest in their prize. In other words, you'll stick around for the romantic tango but will be out the door once the fire dims. **Commitment means nothing if the sparks aren't flying.**

As a Fire sign, Aries needs someone who's equally passionate and charismatic. Otherwise, you're not into it. End of story. Romance with an Aries involves lots of excitement: dancing, partying, hiking, water skiing, even rock climbing!

If you're dating an Aries, you might need to toughen up, because impulsive Aries are quick to lose their tempers (and just as quick to calm down). Life with them can sometimes be an emotional roller-coaster ride—thrilling and fun, but borderline scary.

Aries's Perfect Love Match

As a Fire sign, Aries is usually attracted to other fire signs—**Leo, Sagittarius,** and **other Aries**—because they can satisfy Aries's craving for constant stimulation. Leo's a winner in the love lottery, as long as Leo and Aries don't end up trying to outdo each other. Aries and Sag make an awesome couple, because you share a live-for-the-moment philosophy. An Aries-to-Aries match-up can be bliss. But watch out—too much fire can be explosive!

The Earth signs—**Taurus, Virgo, and Capricorn**—can help ground Aries's frenetic energy . . . if they don't smother the flames. Taurus's laid-back nature can teach Aries a much-needed lesson in patience. Virgo's no-nonsense practicality just might show the Ram a thing or two about what *really* matters in life—if the relationship lasts past that initial awkward stage. Capricorn's need for stability can calm impulsive Aries (*somebody's* got to) . . . or drive her psycho.

The sensitive Water signs—**Cancer, Scorpio, and Pisces**—aren't the best match-up for in-your-face Aries, but they've been known to work. Though Cancer has the ability to reach deep down into the hidden depths of Aries's soul, the Ram's not into touchy-feely emotional stuff. Scorpio's smoldering emotions can ignite—or burn out—Aries's explosive feelings. Hooking up with mystical Pisces can give Aries the satisfaction of nonjudgmental love, if the Ram's nurture-shy nature doesn't send the Fish swimming to safer waters.

Aries can get into the mind power of the Air signs—**Gemini, Libra, and Aquarius**. There's never a dull moment with airhead Gemini, who knows how to stimulate Aries's brain. Independent Aquarius keeps Aries's love of the hunt alive and well. And Libra, Aries's opposite sign in the sky, can be an instant soul mate (or an immediate turnoff).

Does he rock your world or bum you out? Check out the Cosmic Love-O-Meter to find out what sign lights your fire.

Cosmic Love-♡-Meter

Aries girl with:

Aries	Taurus	Gemini	Cancer	Leo	Virgo	Libra	Scorpio	Sag	Cap	Aqu	Pisces
💋	🤝	💥	🚫	💋	🚫	💥	🚫	💋	🤝	💥	🤝

- 💋 Pucker Up—Hot and Heavy Hook-Up
- 🤝 Holding Hands—Born to Be Buds
- 💥 Explosive Combo—Watch Out!
- 🚫 Stay Away—Or Else

Do You Root for Rams?

So you've snagged yourself a Ram. Here's some stuff you should know:

Three Ways to Get a Ram's Attention:
1. Act (and be) self-confident.
2. Be big-time physical. Rams aren't into girls who sit on the sidelines.
3. Don't blend in with the crowd. Wear something unique!

All-time Fave Ram Dates:
1. Play video games together (loser buys lunch!).
2. Spend bucks on each other at the mall.
3. Play any kind of sports together.

Classic Ram Guy-Flicks:
1. *Terminator*
2. *Braveheart*
3. Any James Bond film

Classic Ram Guy Music:
1. Beastie Boys
2. Limp Bizkit
3. D'Angelo (only when his buds aren't around)

You and your Ram have had a fight. The best ways to make up are:
1. Smile at him when you see him in the hall.
2. Sing "your song" at the next karaoke party.
3. Leave a gift on his doorstep with a note that says, "I'm sorry."

Super Ram Anniversary Gifts:
1. After one month: a bright red mug with your name on it
2. After six months: a survival knife/tool kit
3. After one year: tickets to a boxing or wrestling match

The Friend Factor

If you're an Aries, you're about as **true-blue** as it gets. You'll stick up for your pal, whether she's 100 percent right or dead-on wrong. You absolutely hate seeing someone treated unfairly. And if the situation gets a bit tense? You're always ready for a good fight. Aries actually enjoys confrontation.

If You're Friends with a Ram:
- Be honest.
- Let her win every once in a while.
- Don't meddle.
- Don't make too many rules.
- Keep life interesting.

But Aries can be a bit self-centered. You can be so involved with your own problems, you don't even notice everyone else's. So you have to make an extra effort to notice your friends' moods.

And you're bossy. Your unofficial motto is, "My way or no way." If you want to keep your friends, do your best to keep that overbearing part of your personality in check!

School, Sports, and Work

Most Aries are good students for two major reasons: First off, thanks to your go-getter attitude, you're pretty sharp. If you don't know how to do something, you make it your business to find out, pronto. And second, you're competitive: Like your sign's symbol, the Ram, **you'll overcome any obstacle to get ahead.**

In school, it's only natural for Aries to love history. Ancient battles and wars fascinate you. Though you're gung-ho about starting new projects, finishing them is a whole other story. But surprise quizzes and last-minute assignments don't fluster you, because you'll take excitement (and a challenge) wherever you can get it.

Since Aries are physical beings, you're natural athletes. You're into all kinds of sports, especially any activity that takes place outdoors. And you love activities that allow you to compete one-on-one, like swimming or gymnastics.

Typical Ram Careers:
- President
- Politician
- Military officer
- Firefighter
- Professional athlete
- Public relations consultant
- Surgeon
- Stock trader

Figuring out what you're going to be when you grow up is sometimes tough because Aries has a hard time narrowing down options. Being around other people will make you happiest—and most successful—so any job in sales, public relations, or the military will satisfy the need to mingle (and be in charge).

Looking Good

Fire-driven Aries is always ready to try the latest runway look, whether it be belly-button jewels or thigh-high boots. And since standing out in a crowd comes naturally to these Mars-driven nonconformists, you can bet your own personal look is worlds apart from your friends'. With hair and makeup, **just about anything goes—just as long as it's eye-catching.**

Aries Fashion Passions

- Looking strong and fit
- Clothes with clean lines to show off your bod
- Dressing to extremes—either really dressed up or way, way casual
- A thorough head-to-toe glance in the mirror before leaving the house (to make sure you're looking fine)
- Lots of bright and shiny accessories (especially earrings and hair clips)

Aries Perfect Party-Down Outfit:
Army pants with a beaded halter top

Taurus

Chapter Two

(April 20 to May 20)

Symbol: The Bull (as in "Stubborn as a . . . !")

Element: Earth (Practical is my middle name.)

Quality: Fixed (about as movable as concrete)

Energy: Feminine/Yin

Ruler: Venus (the goddess of charm)

Color: Sweet baby blue and soft, cuddly pale pink

Gem: Emerald

Keywords: Reliable, artistic, resourceful

Flower: Rose, poppy

Celebrity Bulls: Cate Blanchett, Cher, George Clooney, Queen Elizabeth II, Audrey Hepburn, Enrique Iglesias, Janet Jackson, Billy Joel, Jack Nicholson, Michelle Pfeiffer, Barbra Streisand, Uma Thurman, Stevie Wonder, Malcolm X, Renee Zellweger

Here Comes the Sun

Nobody's more sensible than a Taurus. With all four feet planted firmly on the ground, the Bull invented the word "practical." You're **reliable, stable, and secure**—and expect the same from everybody who inhabits your world. Okay, as the Zodiac's first Fixed sign, Taureans are not the most flexible of people. It will be a music-free day at MTV before you do anything you don't want to do. But you *can* listen to reason—just as long as you're presented with all the facts.

Bulls are methodical thinkers who use a very special formula to arrive at a decision. You take your time to listen, absorb, and ponder—and only then do you decide what's right. Luckily, you have endless patience.

But there's way more to a Bull than all of that practical stuff. Don't forget that your ruler is luxury-loving Venus. Material things mean a lot to Taurus, for both their sentimental value and their net worth. Bulls like having lots of pretty things around them (including good-looking humans of both the male and female variety).

Bulls can be one of the Zodiac's most charming and affectionate creatures—when you get your way, that is. When you don't, you can be sullen, introverted, and unreasonable. But all

Bull Likes:
- Security in all shapes and forms
- Knowing what to expect
- Shopping
- Watching TV
- Being in love

Bull Dislikes:
- Change
- Being jealous
- Weakness (both emotional and physical)
- Having to rush
- People who don't return what they've borrowed

is forgiven the moment you open your mouth—thanks to Venus, the planet of speech, song, and musical genius. When you're in the mood, the world had better watch out. **You can charm the 501s off anyone.**

Taurus in Love

Bulls are *sooo* into love. Taurus creatures like **good old-fashioned romance**—a candlelit dinner, a walk on the beach, holding hands in the park. Just about every romantic cliché ever invented turns you on. And once you find love, you do your best to hold on to it, no matter what. So if anyone tries to undermine your love relationship, they'd better watch out! A jealous Bull is not a pretty sight.

Bulls believe in physical attraction, big time. But that's not to say you think looks are everything. Taurus is one of the few signs that isn't into physical perfection. If you have to choose between a regular guy who's got a load of charisma, or a major hunk who's oh-so-dull, bachelor number one's the guy for you.

Wooing a Bull is amazingly easy. Be charming, thoughtful, and laugh at their jokes. Give them some physical attention (a neck rub or back scratching will get you far) and you'll have the big, bad Bull eating out of your hand.

What they won't stand for is deceit and betrayal, no matter what. **Bulls believe that promises are made to be kept.** Break a pledge and you break their trust. Forever.

Taurus's Perfect Love Match

Earthbound Taurus feels good around the other Earth signs—**Virgo, Capricorn, and Taurus**—because you're all on the same wavelength. You feel right at home with loving, sensible Virgo, and that's always a good thing. A Capricorn sweetie is good for the Bull, because you share the same values. And putting two Bulls together doubles the pleasure and doubles the fun. But since hooking Earth up with Earth can also double the practicality, big-time attraction can sometimes disappear.

When it comes to the Air signs—**Gemini, Libra, and Aquarius**—it's a mixed bag. Gemini's flightiness can either make solid Taurus freak out or show you how to relax, and Aquarius's "Who cares what they think" attitude is something the status-conscious Bull can't relate to. Sharing Venus as their ruler makes Taurus and Libra both crave romance and affection. But you may not have anything in common besides lots of kissing potential.

Fire signs can teach Taurus how to live the wild life. **Leo** can definitely show the Bull a good time, if both signs are able to give up control (and that's a mighty big if). **Sagittarius's** love of the outdoors can keep you both busy, but romance might be missing in the long run. With **Aries,** you can (finally) learn how to let go, but only if you can get beyond the Ram's bossy demeanor.

Taurus digs the sensitive vibe of the Water signs—**Cancer, Scorpio, and Pisces**. Sweet Cancer is the perfect sign for you to play house with, because you both crave security. With Taurus's opposite sign, Scorpio, the love level reaches a smoldering point. You're kissing-compatible, for sure, but you've also met your match in stubbornness. It takes an intuitive sign like Pisces to convince Bulls to let down their guard. And when you finally do, it's pure heaven.

Does he rock your world or bum you out? Check out the Cosmic Love-O-Meter to find out what sign lights your fire.

Cosmic Love-♡-Meter

Taurus girl with:

Aries	Taurus	Gemini	Cancer	Leo	Virgo	Libra	Scorpio	Sag	Cap	Aqu	Pisces
Explosive	Holding Hands	Stay Away	Pucker Up	Explosive	Holding Hands	Pucker Up	Explosive	Stay Away	Holding Hands	Stay Away	Pucker Up

 Pucker Up—
Hot and Heavy
Hook-Up

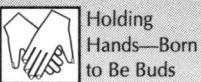 Holding
Hands—Born
to Be Buds

 Explosive
Combo—
Watch Out!

 Stay Away
—Or Else

Do You Brake for Bulls?

So you've snagged yourself a Bull. Here's some essential stuff you should know:

Three Ways to Get a Bull's Attention:

❶ Compliment him.
❷ Wear clothes that fit in with the crowd (nothing too unusual).
❸ Talk to him about music (Taurus digs just about any kind).

All-time Fave Bull Dates:

❶ Hang around on the couch watching TV (and eating popcorn . . . with butter).
❷ Play Monopoly together (let him be the banker).
❸ Go on a picnic (remember to bring lots of food!).

Classic Bull Guy-Flicks:

❶ *Three Kings*
❷ *American Pie*
❸ Any movie that started out as a TV show

Classic Bull Guy Music:

❶ Creed
❷ Dave Matthews Band
❸ Old Motown (Temptations, Marvin Gaye, Al Green, Four Tops)

You and your Bull have had a fight. The best ways to make up are:

❶ Send an "I'm sorry" message to his beeper.
❷ Bake him some brownies.
❸ E-mail him a music clip download of his favorite tune.

Super Bull Anniversary Gifts:

❶ After one-month: a solid chocolate heart!
❷ After six-months: a baby-soft sweater you knit yourself
❸ After one-year: a teeny-tiny TV to take with him everywhere!

The Friend Factor

A Taurus bud is the **ultimate faithful friend**. You'll do anything for your best buds, and they love you for it.

Okay, so the Bull can be a bit of a stick-in-the-mud. If your friends are looking to do anything outside the norm, especially if it's something that can get you in trouble, you're not

If You're Friends with a Bull:

- Be patient.
- Never give a cheap gift.
- Snack with her.
- Be on time. (Being late makes her freak!)
- Never ever embarrass her.

into it. Spying on crushes and making prank calls aren't your idea of a good time.

The Bull's picture should be next to the word **"stubborn"** in the dictionary. Sometimes your friends have trouble getting you to see their side of the story. And Bulls are sticklers for honesty. But if your buds share your passion for integrity and dependability, you'll be friends forever.

School, Sports, and Work

As a practical Earth sign, **Taurus learns by doing**. For you, watching someone install a computer game is way better than reading how to do it from a manual. The same goes with schoolwork. You like to take notes in class, because the process of writing the information down helps your brain absorb it.

Though Bulls are good students who like to be prepared, you totally dread pop quizzes. Another test-taking bummer: timed exams. Bulls do not do their best work under pressure.

Sportswise, Tauruses like activities that show off your Bull-like strength. Being a team player makes sense to Bulls, because you understand how different people, despite their strengths and weaknesses, can join together to form a united group.

When it comes to choosing a grown-up career, Taurus is sure of one thing: **You want a steady home base.** Whether you work from

Typical Bull Careers:
- Banker
- Engineer
- Insurance agent
- Gardener/ landscaper
- Brewer/ winemaker
- Organic farmer
- Masseuse
- Sports coach
- Singer
- Boutique owner

your family room or commute to an office building, you feel best in a day-to-day routine in a familiar environment. And once you find a job you like, you usually stay put. After all, why mess up a good thing?

Looking Good

Sensuous Venus-ruled Bulls crave luxury. When it comes to clothes and jewelry, you want the **real deal**. One mega-expensive cashmere sweater will make you happier than six cheapo ones, and you're drawn to real gold, silver, and gems—except when it comes to chokers. Bulls don't care whether it's a $1.99 special or straight off the Paris runway. If it circles the neck, you've got to have it.

Taurus Fashion Passions

- Anything that feels good on the skin
- Soft and feminine makeup and hair
- An overstuffed closet (so there's *always* something to wear)
- Classic separates and status items mixed with some of the season's latest trends
- Scarves and shawls to throw over any outfit

Taurus Perfect Party-Down Outfit:
Suede skirt, embroidered denim jacket, and a beaded choker

Gemini

Chapter Three

(May 21 to June 20)

Symbol: The Twins (split personality = double the charm)
Element: Air (I think, therefore I am.)
Quality: Mutable (Adaptability is my middle name.)
Energy: Masculine/Yang
Ruler: Mercury (the fast-thinking messenger)
Color: All the colors of the rainbow, but especially yellow
Gem: Agate
Keywords: Quick-witted, inventive, restless
Flower: Lily, lavender

Celebrity Twins: George Bush Sr., Naomi Campbell, Courteney Cox Arquette, Johnny Depp, Rupert Everett, Anne Frank, Sigmund Freud, Judy Garland, Lauryn Hill, Helen Hunt, Angelina Jolie, John F. Kennedy, Tara Lipinski, Paul McCartney, Marilyn Monroe, Alanis Morissette, Mike Myers, Mary-Kate and Ashley Olsen, Natalie Portman

Here Comes the Sun

Certainly you've heard the term "Jack of all trades"? Well, you can bet that expression was coined for someone born under the sign of the Twins. **Being able to do a zillion things** is a blessing . . . and a curse. A blessing because you can finish a test in two seconds flat, sometimes before anyone else even has a chance to read it. A curse because Geminis have such fast-paced brains they sometimes skip over the important stuff—like the instructions.

Ever inquisitive, Geminis need to know the reasons for everything. You are always alert, always interested, and always asking questions. **Changing your mind is a given with Twins.** But that very changeability makes you sharp and effervescent—and witty. Sarcasm, puns, and needle-sharp banter are Gemini trademarks. Which may explain why so many Gems are writers, satirists, and comedians.

On the downside, you can be impractical and fickle, impatient and manipulative. And no sign in the Zodiac is as easily bored as a Twin (as your history teacher is painfully aware). That's why Geminis like to have lots of background noise, whether from the TV, radio, or stereo.

Twin Likes:
- Reading
- Talking (to anybody)
- The freedom to move around
- Doing two or three or four things at once
- Traveling

Twin Dislikes:
- Boredom
- Being told what to do
- Anything ordinary or status quo
- Anything final
- Wasting time

Communication keeps a Twin alive. Cut off contact to the outside world and it's Snore City. That's why you need a constant diet of magazines, movies, and talk shows. And nobody loves trivia as much as a Gemini. You know all that quasi-useless information that's flying around the cosmos? It eventually ends up in the brain of a Twin.

Gemini in Love

How do Geminis love? Let me count the ways. . . . If you're a Twin, you believe in the concept of love, big time. Somewhere in the universe you know there's a soul mate waiting just for you—and it's up to you to find him. So you spend a lot of time flirting, wearing eye-catching outfits, and saying clever things—all in the name of finding *the* one.

Once a Gem finds the right one (or thinks she has), the searching questions start. "What would you do if. . . ?" and "How would you feel if I. . . ?" These questions have to be tough because you require a partner who's on the same wavelength as you are. Otherwise you lose interest asap.

Okay, so you and your honey can communicate via ESP and love exactly the same bands. But aligning your brain is only half the battle. **A Gemini in love demands complete freedom** or all bets are off. And we're talking the freedom to flirt whenever the mood strikes. (But if you're in love with a Gemini, don't expect the same laid-back treatment. If a Gemini sees your eyes wandering, the relationship is history.)

If you're lucky enough to hook up with a Twin, it'll be excitement every single day. Mediocrity doesn't cut it with these nimble-brained individuals. They love adventure and surprises. There's one thing you can expect if you're snuggling down with a Gemini. Yep, you guessed it: **the unexpected**.

Gemini's Perfect Love Match

When Air-ruled Gemini joins up with another Air sign—**Libra, Aquarius, or another Gemini**—you can bet there'll be a lot of hoarse voices by the end of the night. That's because when these signs get together, it's a regular talk-a-thon. With chatterbox Libra, Gemini can find someone who's equally clever *and* romantic. Unique Aquarius can help to expand Gemini's horizons, if you ever stop arguing about which hip-hop band rules the music world. When a Twin joins up with another Twin, it's a whirlwind of amusement. With nonstop gabbing and kissing, this relationship's all about the mouth.

Laid-back Earth signs—**Virgo, Capricorn, and Taurus**—can spark some genuine Gemini interest. Virgo can get into your head better than almost anybody, but Virgo's shyness can prevent a solid love connection from forming. Capricorn's quiet conservatism can drive you mad, or keep you challenged. While a dose of Taurus's inflexibility can actually be mucho stimulating, once you get over the initial head-butting.

When it comes to the game of love, an Air-Water twosome usually scores in the fair to moderate zone. **Cancer's** hardcore emotions can overwhelm brainiac Gemini. Mega-intense **Scorpio** can have a hard time dealing with the Twin's preference for keeping things light. And **Pisces** is way too sweet and sincere to handle Gemini's biting wit and sarcasm.

You know how fire needs plenty of air in order to burn? Well, the same principle applies when you put airy Gemini with any of the Fire signs—**Leo, Sagittarius, or Aries**. Cocky Leo likes having a good time just as much as Gemini does, so you can be sure this combo will stir up plenty of wild times. Gemini's opposite sign, Sagittarius, is sure to spark a love/hate connection. And Aries's what-you-see-is-what-you-get attitude turns challenge-obsessed Gemini on, big time.

Does he rock your world or bum you out? Check out the Cosmic Love-O-Meter to find out what sign lights your fire.

Cosmic Love-♡-Meter

Gemini girl with:

Aries	Taurus	Gemini	Cancer	Leo	Virgo	Libra	Scorpio	Sag	Cap	Aqu	Pisces
💋	🤝	💥	🚫	💋	🤝	💋	🚫	💥	🚫	💋	🤝

 Pucker Up—Hot and Heavy Hook-Up

 Holding Hands—Born to Be Buds

 Explosive Combo—Watch Out!

 Stay Away—Or Else

Do You Have a Thirst for Twins?

So you've snagged yourself a Twin. Here's some essential stuff you should know:

Three Ways to Get a Twin's Attention:

❶ Say something witty.
❷ Talk to him about current events and celebrity gossip.
❸ Be smart (Gemini is turned on by a big brain!).

All-time Fave Twin Dates:

❶ Play Scrabble or Trivial Pursuit (just about any word game will do).
❷ Go to the movies (the less commercial the flick, the better).
❸ Hang out at the bookstore looking through the tabloids.

Classic Twin Guy-Flicks:
❶ *Scream 3* (the film-within-a-film amazes Gemini)
❷ *The Sting*
❸ Anything with subtitles

Classic Twin Guy Music:
❶ Pearl Jam
❷ Lenny Kravitz
❸ Any obscure musical artist that nobody's ever heard of

You and your Twin have had a fight. The best ways to make up are:
❶ Send him an apology in rhyme.
❷ Call him on the phone (Twins can spend hours chatting away).
❸ Mail him a bizarre postcard that reads "Oops!"

Super Twin Anniversary Gifts:
❶ After one month: a grab bag of gags (the cornier the better)
❷ After six months: a leather-bound journal
❸ After one year: a cell phone

The Friend Factor

Gemini needs lots of friends to play with. No one loves games more than a Twin—board games, sports, head games—anything to keep your ever-spinning brain from becoming bored.

One of your favorite things to do is sharing your innermost thoughts with your best buds—

If You're Friends with a Gemini:
- Be funny.
- Talk and think fast.
- Don't complain to her.
- Keep her in the loop (no one hates not knowing what's going on like a Twin).
- Be open to new ideas.

and listening to theirs. It takes a lot to shock you, which is why your friends know they can tell you their most embarrassing personal stories and you won't bat an eye. **No concept or dream is too far-out for a Twin to handle.**

If you're friends with a Gemini, you should be aware that she tends to be late, because the whole concept of time is way too boring for her. And her nonstop flirting can become a bit tiresome. But still, she's a one-in-a-million Gem(ini).

School, Sports, and Work

Gemini's brain cells are constantly working overtime, much to the amazement of your slower-thinking buds and teachers. You learn through **constant mental stimulation and lots of variety**.

The Gemini mind soaks up obscure facts like a sponge, which is why most trivia champs are born in late May and June. One of your strongest talents is languages. Natural mimics, Twins easily pick up foreign tongues. And it's a rare Gemini who doesn't have the gift of perfect grammar.

As far as activities go, Geminis are into sports that give your lungs a workout. The aerobics craze was probably invented by a Twin, because you like sports that require a lot of breathing. You also love exercising while you're doing something else. You can't jog

Typical Twin Careers:
- Reporter
- Gossip columnist
- Advertising
- Salesperson
- Translator
- Travel writer
- Travel agent
- DJ or VJ
- Illustrator

without headphones on or use a Stairmaster without flipping through a mag at the same time.

Choosing a career can be really hard, because **Geminis are equally good at a lot of things**. The trick for a Twin is to remember that whatever you choose, you don't have to be stuck doing it forever. Whatever you do to pay the bills, it's got to give you freedom and the ability to meet lots of people, or it won't be satisfying.

Looking Good

When it comes to fashion, **Gemini will try anything once**. Hairpieces and extensions? Yup. Red mascara? Sure. If it's in the latest fashion mag, the Twins are into it. The outfits you choose reflect your outgoing and offbeat personality, and the concept of the plain little black dress is alien to you—unless you decorate it with earrings, necklaces, bracelets, and rings.

Gemini Fashion Passions

- Accessories, accessories, and more accessories
- Silver-tone jewelry and hair ornaments
- Ultrabright colors and funky prints
- A beltpack or backpack ('cause you're always on the go!)
- Wearable art

Gemini Perfect Party-Down Outfit:
A multi-hued sarong skirt, tank top, rings on your fingers and toes, and a flower in your hair

Cancer

Chapter Four

(June 21 to July 22)

Symbol: The Crab (celestial homebody)

Element: Water (I can sense an emotion a mile away!)

Quality: Cardinal (Well, *someone's* gotta be in charge.)

Energy: Feminine/Yin

Ruler: The Moon (the source of your legendary moods)

Color: Silvery, lunar gray

Gem: Pearl

Keywords: Intuitive, compassionate, protective

Flowers: Water lily, jasmine

Celebrity Crabs: Beck, Tom Cruise, John Cusack, Harrison Ford, Frida Kahlo, Helen Keller, Michelle Kwan, Pamela Anderson Lee, Courtney Love, Tia and Tamera Mowry, Chris O'Donnell, Prince William, Princess Diana, Liv Tyler, Robin Williams, Meryl Streep

Here Comes the Sun

Though Cancers appear to be quiet and skittish, just like your symbol the Crab, underneath your shell you're full of emotion and intensity. You have to feel comfortable before you reveal your true self. In fact, **being secure and comfy may be Cancer's most important requirement for enjoying life**.

Cancers are kind and observant and can pick up on anybody's mood in a nanosecond. Family and honor mean a lot to Moon Children. You adore your mom and dad and possess a natural-born instinct for dealing with mischievous toddlers (which is probably why you always find yourself baby-sitting for friends and neighbors).

Basically, you're into anything old, which may explain why you live for thrift stores and tag sales. And you're definitely obsessive about keepsakes. Chances are you still have the ticket stub from the first movie you ever saw.

Whipping up meals out of nowhere is something you're born knowing how to do. Forget about vending machines. You're into real food—stuff that's actually made of organic ingredients. The downside to Crabs? **Nobody's moodier.** One minute, you're ready to rock,

Crab Likes:
- Hanging at home
- Looking at old photos
- Antiques
- Protecting the weak
- Daydreaming

Crab Dislikes:
- Hurtful people
- Standing out in a crowd
- Not having enough (of anything)
- Being unloved
- Leaving home

and the next, you'd rather stay home and rest. But with any luck your Crabbiness doesn't last long, and you come out of your shell in no time.

Cancer in Love

Moon Kids in love are **extremely affectionate**. Most of you are into pet names and baby talk (come on, admit it). When you're with your one and only, you have to have some physical contact or you go crazy.

As a Water sign, Cancers love being near H_2O. A trip to the beach or a boat ride are favorite Crab date scenes. If you can't get near a body of water, a walk in the rain will do in a pinch.

How do you pair up with a Cancer? Take things nice and slow. After an acceptable waiting period, make the first move. Crabs can be so frightened of being rejected, it can take forever for them to pledge their undying devotion. And don't tease Crabs right away, or they'll withdraw back into their protective shell.

The best recipe for getting a Moon Kid to open up is very simple. Start out with a healthy dose of affection. Add a romantic setting (candlelight and stars will do) and a heartfelt token of your love, and the result will be divine. And since Crabs are so **kind and tender**, you know the experience will be worth the wait!

Cancer's Perfect Love Match

A water-to-water connection is always good, because emotions rule, all around. With another **Cancer**, there will be lots of soul-baring, but since you're both couch potatoes, you'll never actually go out and *do* anything. **Scorpio's** intensity is a definite turn-on, but their possessiveness can leave you feeling claustrophobic. **Pisces** just might be Cancer's number-one soul mate, but you can both get caught up in life's sorrows and inequities.

The go-get-'em action of the Fire signs—**Leo, Sagittarius, and Aries**—can be way too intense for gentle spirit Cancer. Leo's strength is that their "Ain't I Wonderful" attitude can rub off on the insecure Crab. Sag's "What You See Is What You Get" point of view is refreshing, because Crabs can't stand a phony. But, still, without that inner spark, they may be better off as friends. The Aries/Cancer connection is usually pretty turbulent. But if they don't mind buckling their emotional seat belt, it can be a fantastic adventure.

When Cancer gets together with the thinking Air signs—**Libra, Aquarius, and Gemini**—the connection is more intellectual than emotional. Romantic Libra is probably the best bet of the three because your snuggling requirements are similar. Ultra-unique Aquarius can be too forward-moving for nostalgic Crabs, and their hesitancy to commit to a relationship could lead Cancer to Dumpsville. Cancer's neighboring sign of Gemini lacks the stability and consistency that Crabs need. But just imagine the fascinating conversations you can have together!

The Earth signs—**Virgo, Capricorn, and Taurus**—are definite lip-locking candidates. Virgo's sweet and subtle way of catering to your every need is a major plus. Way over in the opposite part of the sky, Capricorn shares Cancer's desire for security and the simple things in life. Affectionate Taurus offers the chance for a hot and heavy love connection—*and* a commitment.

Does he rock your world or bum you out? Check out the Cosmic Love-O-Meter to find out what sign lights your fire.

Do You Crush on Crabs?

So you've snagged yourself a Crab. Here's some essential stuff you should know:

Three Ways to Get a Crab's Attention:

1. Act shy.
2. Wear something feminine (baggy sweats are a no-no!).
3. Be attentive to his needs.

All-time Fave Crab Dates:

1. Go to the beach (any body of water will do).
2. Share some food together (if it's homemade, you score extra!).
3. Go to a museum or antique store (Crabs love old stuff).

Classic Crab Guy-Flicks:

1. *Forrest Gump*
2. *The Nutty Professor* (the Eddie Murphy remake)
3. Anything historical (especially having to do with the Civil War)

Classic Crab Guy Music:

1. Grateful Dead
2. Phish
3. Any old-time vinyl recordings (the scratchier the better)

You and your Crab have had a fight. The best ways to make up are:

1. Pass him an "I'm sorry" note in the hall.
2. Ask his brother or sister to talk to him about how sorry you are.
3. Wear a piece of his clothing to school.

Super Crab Anniversary Gifts:

1. After one month: a handmade card (he'll treasure it forever)
2. After six months: a photo album of the two of you
3. After one year: an inflatable boat

The Friend Factor

Moon Kids make some of the best friends. **You're great listeners and expert problem-solvers**. And since you're so family-oriented, you treat your true-blue buds like sisters (and expect the same from them).

You have an extra-special ability to make other people feel ultracomfortable, even if

If You're Friends with a Crab:

- Be sensitive.
- Respect her traditional values.
- Eat her chow.
- Treat her like family.
- Take her to the nearest flea market.

you've only just met each other. In fact, the new kid at school is usually befriended by a Crab, because it hurts you to see *anyone* looking lonely.

Your feelings are easily hurt, too. Unfortunately, your powerful emotions, especially when combined with a healthy dose of PMS, can make you ultrasensitive. **Good friends need to give you lots of reassurance**.

School, Sports, and Work

Cancer's academic specialties include a wide range of subjects, from history to astronomy to poetry. Because you take everything personally, **you learn best by relating**—getting inside the heads of the people behind an event. You love biographies because you like to know what makes people tick.

Cancers are one of the few signs that don't live for sports. Sure, you dig communing with Mother Nature, but rugged sports like football and soccer don't interest you. If you're going to get physical, it will be on the water—by swimming, canoeing, or windsurfing.

Work is something that comes naturally to Crabs, and it's rare to find one who doesn't snag an after-school job. When you do get a job, your workplace needs to be a home-away-from-home, complete with family photos and other personal touches to help provide that Crab sense of security.

Typical Crab Careers:
- Chef
- Antiques restorer
- Museum curator
- Psychotherapist
- Nutritionist
- Boat builder/restorer
- Pediatrician

Looking Good

Lunar-ruled Cancer gals go for a 100-percent-feminine look. Vintage clothes (get this gal to a thrift store, pronto!) are one of the Crab's fashion musts. Anything that reflects your fascination with old-world traditions and completes the retro look will eventually find its way into your closet.

Cancer Fashion Passions

- Clothes with lots of buttons and hooks (old period clothes make you swoon!)
- Heirloom jewelry (especially pearls)
- Subtle feminine makeup
- Hair that's pulled up in a bun or French twist
- Anything that cinches the waist

Cancer Perfect Party-Down Outfit:
Waist-cinching dress from the '50s with a vintage silk wrap and ropes of pearls

Leo

Chapter Five

(July 23 to August 22)

Symbol: The Lion (Hear her roar!)
Element: Fire (which fuels your blazing energy)
Quality: Fixed (Just let 'em try to change your mind.)
Energy: Masculine/Yang
Ruler: The Sun (the center of our solar system . . . which is exactly how you like it!)
Color: Shimmering gold and flaming orange
Gem: Ruby (July Lions) and peridot (August Lions)
Keywords: Magnetism, inner strength, fun-loving
Flower: Sunflower, marigold

Celebrity Lions: Ben Affleck, Gillian Anderson, Lucille Ball, Halle Berry, Sandra Bullock, Bill Clinton, Robert DeNiro, David Duchovny, Woody Harrelson, Whitney Houston, Mick Jagger, Lisa Kudrow, Jennifer Lopez, Madonna, Napoleon, Edward Norton, Jacqueline Kennedy Onassis, Sean Penn, Arnold Schwarzenegger, Martha Stewart

Here Comes the Sun

Introducing . . . the astro-sign supreme, the "it" girl of the Zodiac, the queen of the universe, Leo! Like your fireball ruler, the Sun, **Leos are usually up front and center stage**, and that's just the way they like it. Luckily, the rest of the world usually feels the same way (Whew!). People of both sexes are drawn to your bold self-confidence, dynamic vibe, and never-ending generosity. And talk about nonstop energy! Leos are likely to star in the school play, run for school office, and organize a sports team for disadvantaged kids after school—all at the same time.

Needless to say, you are the **original party person**. You can lead the gang on the dance floor and are equally at ease throwing your own fabulous bash!

Leo is a fixed sign, so behind that warm exterior lurks a stubborn and opinionated person. You are notorious for not budging an inch once your mind is made up. But your friends like and trust you because you speak your mind and stick up for what's right. You are also known for being totally loyal and trustworthy. Your pals had better be there for you, too!

Let's admit it—Lions can also be conceited and ultrademanding. You honestly don't mean

Lion Likes:
- Having a photo taken (and looking at the results)
- Having fun (with a capital F)
- Being adored
- Partying
- Being surrounded by luxury

Lion Dislikes:
- Being ignored
- Deceitful behavior
- Being weak or sick
- Boredom
- Competition (especially if you're losing)

to show off, but you were born to be the center of attention. **Like your ruler, the Sun, you live to shine.**

Leo in Love

Leos love being in love. In fact, you love the whole dating ritual: the search, the flirtation, the first date. It's no surprise that **you're amazingly good at snagging a sweetheart**. I mean, what's not to like about you?

Generous and warmhearted, Leos shower their special someone with cards and gifts, mixing them a special CD, or baking them a batch of cookies. Of course, you expect lots of gifts in return—and **loads** of attention. Hey—anyone who doesn't treat you right can always be replaced.

Because fire fuels their blood, Leos are always active. Having fun is one of your main goals in life. Amusement parks and pro ball games are just a few of the energetic outings that keep you going. And since nobody likes a wild time more than Leo, **you had better find someone who likes parties just as much as you do**.

If you're involved with a Leo, be prepared to witness lots of extracurricular flirting. And no, it doesn't change, even when you become a couple. You see, Lions like lots of attention—from **everyone**. So rather than freaking out, just hold his hand a little tighter. That's how to keep a Lion purring.

Leo's Perfect Love Match

When Leo mixes with the other Fire signs—**Sag, Aries, and Leo**—it's potentially dangerous, but totally stimulating. Fun-loving

Sagittarius makes a fabulous match, because you both live for the wild life. But over the long run this fire may burn itself out. With Aries, the action-oriented energy is right, but the one-upmanship can get to be a real pain. A Leo-to-Leo coupling can really heat things up . . . if you don't mind having to compliment each other 24-7.

The Water signs—**Scorpio, Pisces, and Cancer**—can add some emotional depth to the Lion's life. With Scorpio, there's plenty of passion—and competitiveness. Pisces's naive dreaminess appeals to Leo, but their passivity can be draining. Leo's astro-neighbor, Cancer, can show Lions a sweet side of love you never knew existed—if you don't scare the Crab away first.

Earth signs **Virgo, Capricorn, and Taurus** can help ground ego-driven Lions. Your border sign, Virgo, can teach you a thing or two about being low-key and humble. Trouble is, you might find yourself dozing off before you absorb the lesson. Capricorn's practicality might be just the thing Leo needs to keep you down to earth—if that's where you want to be. Taurus shares Leo's love of the finer things in life. But be forewarned: It'll be you who ends up spending the money.

Leo's best chance at a perfect hook-up is with the more cerebral Air signs—**Libra, Aquarius, and Gemini**. Libra's charm will definitely catch Leo's eye (and mind). And because you're both into compliments, this Venus-ruled sweetie could provide an eternity of flattery. Independent Aquarius is a terrific match for intense Leo, because Aquarius is secure enough to give the Lion some space. And Leos should definitely check out flirtatious Gemini. You both love to talk and party, big time!

Does he rock your world or bum you out? Check out the Cosmic Love-O-Meter to find out what sign lights your fire.

Cosmic Love-♡-Meter

Leo girl with:

| Aries | Taurus | Gemini | Cancer | Leo | Virgo | Libra | Scorpio | Sag | Cap | Aqu | Pisces |

 Pucker Up—Hot and Heavy Hook-Up

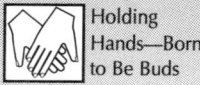 Holding Hands—Born to Be Buds

 Explosive Combo—Watch Out!

 Stay Away—Or Else

Do You Like Lions?

So you've snagged yourself a Lion. Here's some essential stuff you should know:

Three Ways to Get a Lion's Attention:
1. Be ultraconfident.
2. Tell him how special he is.
3. Be flirtatious but hard-to-get at the same time.

All-time Fave Lion Dates:
1. Get your picture taken together in a photo booth.
2. Go to an art gallery or play (especially if it's trendy).
3. Do karaoke together.

Classic Lion Guy-Flicks:

❶ *Shaft*
❷ *Titanic* (only if his friends don't find out about it)
❸ Anything about royalty ('cause that's what he thinks he is)

Classic Lion Guy Music:

❶ Red Hot Chili Peppers
❷ Old Led Zeppelin (the most classic of classic rock)
❸ Broadway tunes (though he'd rather die than admit it)

You and your Lion have had a fight. The best ways to make up are:

❶ Dedicate a song to him on your favorite radio station.
❷ Ask him what you can do to make things all right again.
❸ Wear that outfit that he loves.

Best Lion Anniversary Gifts:

❶ After one month: an hour-long massage
❷ After six months: a gold-plated key chain with his initials
❸ After one year: a singing telegram

The Friend Factor

As the unofficial royal Princess of the Zodiac, you can't help but rule. You know that half of being fabulous is actually *believing* you are, and you're really good at letting your best friends in on the secret. You want them to be the best they can be, too.

As a Lion, **you're there for your friends**. If

If You're Friends with a Lion:

- Be honest and loyal.
- Spoil her.
- Be appreciative.
- Introduce her to all kinds of exotic food (and let her share from your plate!).
- Take her picture.

they're short on cash, you'll buy them lunch. If your best bud's got a crush on that cute linebacker, you'll introduce them at the postgame bash.

Your friends have to be able to handle your high level of self-assurance. Let's face it—watching a Lion shine (and shine and shine) can get awfully tiresome. But friends who are happy to give you that extra C.P.C. (Constant Praise and Compliments) will have someone they can count on through thick and thin.

School, Sports, and Work

You know the kid at school who's constantly waving her arm at the teacher? That's a Leo. She's waving partly because she knows the answer—but mostly because she hates to be cooped up inside the classroom. **The Lion learns best by doing.**

Leos are usually partial to the liberal arts. Drama, painting, and music bring out your inner artist. Creative writing and languages are more of your favorite subjects. Don't be surprised if you end up as captain of the debate team.

Because they're such physical creatures, Lions are totally into sports. It's a rare Leo who doesn't spend a lot of time in a gym. For you, working out is a serious occupation.

Leos usually choose careers that will give you control and allow you to strut your stuff.

Typical Lion Careers:
- Movie producer
- Actor
- Supermodel
- Professional athlete
- Talent agent
- President of the United States
- Restaurant owner
- Motivational speaker

Sure, lots of signs say they'd like to be famous, but Lions really mean it. And given Leo's focus and determination, living large is a dream that could very well turn into reality.

Looking Good

Glamour is the Lion's game, whether you're strutting down the school hallway or turning heads on the dance floor. Bright colors, sexy separates, and look-at-me hair are what keep Leo feeling and looking fab. If it's fit for a queen, it'll work just fine for a Lion.

Leo Fashion Passions

- Jewelry that's 18K gold, with big stones
- Funky temporary hair color
- Flashy makeup trends (Where did you *get* that gold glitter eyeshadow?!)
- Outfits that focus the attention on *you* (which is just how you like it)
- Designer-brand anything

Leo Perfect Party-Down Outfit:
Bright satin minidress with rock-star platforms

Virgo

Chapter Six

(August 23 to September 22)

Symbol: The Virgin (I aim to please)
Element: Earth (straight to the point, and no-frills)
Quality: Mutable (versatile . . . within reason)
Energy: Feminine/Yin
Ruler: Mercury (the source of your discriminating mind)
Color: Navy blue (a fashion classic)
Gem: Sapphire
Keywords: Critical, efficient, matter-of-fact
Flower: Morning glory, azalea

Celebrity Virgins: Tori Amos, Fiona Apple, Sean Connery, Macaulay Culkin, Cameron Diaz, Hugh Grant, Michael Jackson, Stephen King, Mother Theresa, Ryan Phillippe, Keanu Reeves, Leann Rimes, Ben Savage, Claudia Schiffer, Jada Pinkett Smith, Shania Twain, Michelle Williams

Here Comes the Sun

 The sign of Virgo has a pretty high reputation to uphold. Your ruling planet, Mercury, has given you a brain that's focused yet flexible (not a typical combination). Virgo is a Mutable Earth sign, which means you're both **adaptable and oh-so-practical**. Walking into a party full of people you've never laid eyes on would freak most people out, but you calmly assess the situation and have a good time.

That outer calm is balanced by a deep intensity. On the inside, Virgins are restless thinkers and planners. You think it's very important to be organized and in control. Sometimes you can imagine things are going wrong when they're really not (some Virgos can be hypochondriacs). **But you're always trying to make the world around you a little bit better.**

For most of you, neatness is key. Sure, some Virgins have bedrooms that look like Dorothy's house after the twister. But for the most part, you're big believers in "a place for everything and everything in its place." Knowing where your possessions are gives you a major sense of security.

Virgin Likes:
- Spending time alone
- Getting organized
- Eating healthy food
- Analyzing people and situations
- Getting a good deal

Virgin Dislikes:
- PDAs
- Using public bathrooms
- Being criticized and/or intimidated
- Not being in control
- Sweating

Virgo in Love

Romance for Virgo is **100 percent honest love and devotion**. Virgins scope out a potential love mate the same way they write an outline for an important school paper—carefully and methodically. Yes, you're picky, picky, and you hate the element of surprise.

When a Virgin is part of a couple, you like to spend time together alone. More than any other sign, Virgos don't need outside distraction when they're in love. And though the Virgin has a bit of a prudish image, when the time is right, your engines run just as deep as your other half.

Virgos are big into hygiene and cleanliness, so make sure your teeth are brushed and your bod is showered before you even *think* of hooking up with the Virgin. Locking lips in a popcorn-and-chewing-gum-infested multiplex just doesn't happen in Virgo-land. When Virgo's ready to snuggle, he'll do it in a clean and attractive setting.

Virgo's Perfect Love Match

Earthy Virgo gets a warm fuzzy feeling with the other Earth signs—**Capricorn, Taurus, and other Virgins**. Conservative Cap shares your laid-back and low-key attitude, so this could be a very comfy twosome. A relationship with Taurus has a lot of potential, just as long as the Bull doesn't mind having a honey who's not always as affectionate as he is. When Virgo snuggles up to another Virgo, absolute perfection is possible. But just imagine the ultrahigh standards!

When it comes to the Air signs—**Libra, Aquarius, and Gemini**—it's a mixed love bag. Virgo's cusp sign, Libra, will appreciate the Virgin's

"I aim to please" quality and your need for clean. Aquarius's rebellious nature may be too much for practical Virgo's status-quo tastes. Gemini can provide an intense brain-to-brain connection that both signs find stimulating but potentially draining.

It's heads up with the rock 'em, sock 'em Fire signs—**Sagittarius, Aries, and Leo**. Though Virgo can be intrigued by Sag's matter-of-fact sex appeal, the let-it-all-hang-out Centaur may end up driving you crazy. Aries is a little too in-your-face for demure Virgo, but sometimes that can only add to the interest level. And it may be hard for the Virgin to bear Leo's look-at-me attitude. But if the Virgin can ignore the Lion's melodrama, this relationship can work.

In the Water signs—**Scorpio, Pisces, and Cancer**—Virgo meets her match. With intense Scorpio, the love connection is strong, sizzling, and potentially life-changing. A Virgo and Pisces lovefest can go either way—pure, unadulterated bliss or total disaster. Much better stars abound with sweet and subtle Cancer. Both of you are into a higher quality of love than most signs can ever experience. Ahh . . .

Does he rock your world or bum you out? Check out the Cosmic Love-O-Meter to find out what sign lights your fire.

Cosmic Love-♡-Meter

Virgo girl with:

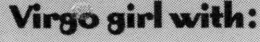

Aries	Taurus	Gemini	Cancer	Leo	Virgo	Libra	Scorpio	Sag	Cap	Aqu	Pisces
🚫	🤝	💥	💋	🚫	💋	🤝	💋	🚫	💋	🤝	💥

 Pucker Up—Hot and Heavy Hook-Up

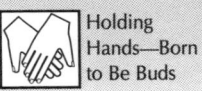 Holding Hands—Born to Be Buds

 Explosive Combo—Watch Out!

 Stay Away—Or Else

Do You Vote for Virgins?

So you've snagged yourself a Virgin. Here's some essential stuff you should know.

Three Ways to Get a Virgin's Attention:
❶ Don't be a show-off.
❷ Be critical of your surroundings (he's the ultimate connoisseur).
❸ Wear outfits that are clean, neat, and unfussy.

All-time Fave Virgin Dates:
❶ Do word puzzles together (crosswords and jumbles especially).
❷ Go to see a foreign film or documentary.
❸ Hang out at a bookstore drinking cappuccino.

Classic Virgin Guy-Flicks:
❶ *10 Things I Hate About You*
❷ *Pulp Fiction* (seeing different perspectives appeals to him big time)
❸ Any Woody Allen film

Classic Virgin Guy Music:
❶ Nine Inch Nails
❷ Green Day
❸ Classical music (and he's not embarrassed to admit it)

You and your Virgin have had a fight. The best ways to make up are:
❶ Send him an e-mail card (but keep it unmushy, please!).
❷ Shake hands and declare a truce.
❸ Do your best not to criticize him personally (even if he does it himself) and you won't have to make up in the first place!

Super Virgin Anniversary Gifts:

1. After one month: a subscription to his fave magazine
2. After six months: some killer computer games
3. After one year: a Palm Pilot

The Friend Factor

Virgos make it their business to be there for their buds. Friends appreciate **your ability to see things as they really are.** You like to tell it like it is, no matter how harsh the reality. Nobody can top your sarcastic sense of humor. And you've got an amazing knack for rooting out someone's bad qualities, which comes in really handy when your friends are too emotionally involved to see the truth.

But as much as Virgo loves to criticize, you can't handle much criticism yourself. That's because, secretly, you can also be insecure. You look for lots of support from your friends—and you're happy to be there for them, too.

If You're Friends with a Virgin:

- Feed her healthy food.
- Be loyal.
- Respect her stuff.
- Help her not to worry.
- Keep her from feeling insecure.

School, Sports, and Work

Virgos are usually brainiacs who rarely freak out about schoolwork. Even if you're assigned a huge project that's due in less than a week, you know how to get the job done without losing your cool. Solving word games and puzzles is relatively simple for you, which may explain why so many of you end up as critics or writers.

Virgo's into English, science, and math. You like any detailed course that stimulates your mind. But that's not to say the Virgin isn't artistic. Whether you sew, paint murals, or garden (and nobody's got a greener thumb than Virgo), you can be sure the result is a work of art.

You won't find a whole lot of jocks and sports-addicts who are Virgins. It's just that you don't like to get all sweaty. Those Virgins who work out do it because it makes them feel and look their best.

The whole career dilemma shouldn't be that stressful for Virgo, because **you know you can cut it, no matter what job you end up with**. And since the Virgin doesn't have an ego problem, you don't freak if you're not the boss. In fact, you're so into serving others that you often prefer to leave the number-one slot to someone else.

Typical Virgin Careers:
- Movie critic
- Landscape designer
- Office manager
- Technical writer
- Diplomat (or spy!)
- Homeopathic doctor
- Health food store owner
- Research scientist

Looking Good

"Keep it grounded and functional" is the Virgin's mantra. Instead of following the latest trend, **Virgo prefers well-tailored separates** that she can wear year after year. Grooming is a prerequisite for these clean freaks, so missing buttons and hanging threads will never be seen on their clothing. Hair-wise, they like simple and sleek looks and spare, barely-there makeup.

Virgo Fashion Passions

- Constant grooming
- Details, details, details (like delicate embroidery and tiny buttons)
- Minimal and discreet accessories (diamond stud earrings will do, thank you!)
- Custom-made anything
- Hypoallergenic makeup (and please don't ask to share)

Virgo Perfect Party-Down Outfit:
Japanese-inspired shift with one knockout piece of jewelry

Libra

Chapter Seven

(September 23 to October 22)

Symbol: The Scales (I weigh it all out.)
Element: Air (the thinking gal's fuel)
Quality: Cardinal
Energy: Masculine/Yang
Ruler: Venus (the fashion stylist planet)
Color: Any color . . . just as long as it's a pastel
Gem: Opal
Keywords: Artistic, refined, opinionated
Flower: Hydrangea, cabbage roses

Celebrity Scales: Neve Campbell, Jimmy Carter, Rachael Leigh Cook, Matt Damon, Snoop Doggy Dog, Michael Douglas, Janeane Garofalo, Jim Henson, Jesse Jackson, John Lennon, Heather Locklear, Groucho Marx, Gwyneth Paltrow, Eleanor Roosevelt, Alicia Silverstone, Will Smith, Gwen Stefani, Barbara Walters, Serena Williams, Kate Winslet, Catherine Zeta-Jones

Here Comes the Sun

 Libra's sign is the Scales, and Scales strive for balance and fairness. **You want the world around you to be harmonious and beautiful**, and when it's not you try to make it that way. A natural diplomat, you bend over backward to see both sides of an issue. Because you're so intent on being fair to everyone, you can sometimes seem indecisive. You have to weigh all the facts until you reach the right decision. Is it any surprise that a lot of Libras are lawyers and judges?

A lover of the arts, **you pride yourself on your good taste and love of beauty**. Like your ruling planet, Venus, you are sophisticated, cultured, and refined. Good manners and good grooming mean a lot to you. It's no wonder the fashion world is filled with Libras, because they are born knowing what looks good.

Like other Air signs, Libra has an active and inquisitive mind, and you love discussing politics, literature, and ideas. Because you are so fair-minded, you don't take it personally when someone disagrees with you. Libras really believe that *everyone* is entitled to his or her own opinion.

Scales Likes:
- Being fair
- Looking good
- Getting her way
- Turning a "before" into an "after"
- Balancing the pros and cons

Scales Dislikes:
- Making up her mind
- Ugly environments
- Direct confrontation
- Prejudice and bigotry
- Being ordinary

Libra in Love

Libra is in love with love itself. **No one is more romantic than a Libra**, and you can spend hours just imagining what the great romance of your life will be like. You're a sucker for love stories. Just the thought of *Titanic*, *Gone With the Wind*, or *Romeo and Juliet* makes you want to burst into tears.

Libras always run the risk of being disappointed. After all, real love seldom lives up to the ideal. But your good sense keeps most Libras from becoming cynical. Even Libras know that most guys don't actually look like Leonardo DiCaprio!

Candlelight and seductive music are part of every bona fide Libra's passionate game plan. You love to cater to your honey's every desire. And talk about devotion: When the two of you are out together, you would never even think of *looking* at another potential mate.

If you're trying to nab a Libra honey, be sure to turn on the charm, because **nobody likes flattery more than Libra**. Major flirting and intense eye contact will almost always work.

Libra's Perfect Love Match

As an Air sign, Libra needs regular mental stimulation. Who better to provide it than one of the other Air signs—**Aquarius, Gemini, or another Libra**? The Water Bearer's unique and unconventional vision appeals to Libra's nontraditional side. With Gemini, Libra will never be without conversation. But you can become so caught up in verbal wordplay that your romance never goes into high gear. A Libra-to-Libra pairing can be sugar-sweet because you both know how to treat each other really well. But will you ever be able to decide upon *anything*?

The Earth signs—**Capricorn, Taurus, and Virgo**—can have a much-needed stabilizing effect on airy Libra. Fellow Cardinal signs Capricorn and Libra share the same "I can make it happen" quality. They can learn a lot from each other, if they can ever stop fighting over who's in charge. With Venus ruling both signs, Taurus and Libra are born to snuggle. Unfortunately, Libra can find Taurus's stubborn streak totally annoying. Libra's neighboring sign, Virgo, is equally intense about giving their all to the one they're into, so this hook-up could be a classic love connection.

The emotional Water signs—**Scorpio, Pisces, and Cancer**—can help bring out Libra's tender side. Scorpio's natural appeal makes it very easy for Libra to be attracted. But the Scorpion's need for control can be a major turn-off for equality-minded Libra. When Pisces and Libra make a pair, it looks like love, but if you peer beneath the surface, it's apparent that Libra's a little scared of the Fish's emotional intensity. With Cancer, Libra's found a lover who worships partnership—and baby talk—just as much as you do.

The heat rises when you pair Libra up with the Fire signs—**Sagittarius, Aries, and Leo**. Sag's easygoing attitude helps Libra relax, and the Scales can get the Centaur to give storybook romance a try. Libra's opposite sign, Aries, can be a match made in heaven . . . or not at all. In Leo, Libra finds somebody who likes giving—and receiving—compliments as much as you do. This love could last forever.

Does he rock your world or bum you out? Check out the Cosmic Love-O-Meter to find out what sign lights your fire.

Do You Seek a Scales?

So you've snagged yourself a Scales. Here's some essential stuff you should know:

Three Ways to Get a Scales' Attention:
❶ Get into a discussion (he loves sharing ideas).
❷ Pick up on one of his special qualities—and compliment him on it.
❸ Be social (he digs a friendly girl).

All-time Fave Scales Dates:
❶ Go to an art museum or gallery (even window displays will do).
❷ Hang out talking about how terrific you both are together.
❸ Scout out a flea market.

Classic Scales Guy-Flicks:

1. *Lethal Weapon* (all of them—he loves movies that feature a team)
2. *Can't Hardly Wait*
3. Any films that feature luxury (he digs eye candy)

Classic Scales Guy Music:

1. Goo-Goo Dolls
2. Prince
3. Lauryn Hill (but only when you're alone)

You and your Scales have had a fight. The best ways to make up are:

1. Send him a handmade "I messed up" card.
2. Write him a funny poem about your big blow-out.
3. Braid him a leather choker as a peace offering.

Super Scales Anniversary Gifts:

1. After one month: a copy of a book he'll love—inscribed with a mushy sentiment, of course!
2. After six months: tickets to the concert he's been dying to see
3. After one year: an I.D. bracelet (engraved with both your initials)

The Friend Factor

Courteous, friendly, and oh so charming, Libra loves having her friends around. As the social goddess of the Zodiac, **you're naturally outgoing and have a rep for being kind and helpful**—especially when it comes to helping your girlfriend snag her crush.

Libra is one of the few signs who can

If You're Friends with a Scales:

- Fuss over her a bit.
- Be patient with her indecisiveness.
- Do lots of girly stuff together.
- Surround her with beauty.
- Allow her to play the peacemaker.

distance herself emotionally from just about any scenario. Your buds love asking you for advice, because your suggestions are completely impartial and just.

Granted, you can be a bit self-absorbed sometimes, and you're a sucker for compliments. And you hate being excluded from anything. Nothing burns you up more than being ignored—you'd rather have someone insult you to your face than act as if you didn't exist!

School, Sports, and Work

Libras dig school but aren't crazy about the work, because they hate to do anything that's expected of them. "Question authority" is your motto, though you're awfully subtle about it.

When it comes to subjects, **most Libras are drawn to the arts**. You spend lots of time in creative writing class, flexing your hamstrings at the ballet bar, or acting your way toward that Academy Award. Lots of Libras get pumped for sports; you just don't usually *live* for them. When you do get physical, nine times out of ten you choose a team sport. Yet for Libra, picking out a flattering outfit just might be more fun than playing the game.

Choosing a career is especially hard for Libra, because decision-making is not your strong suit. **Any profession that allows you to act as a referee—like marriage counselor,**

Typical Scales Careers:
- Ambassador
- Window dresser
- Portrait photographer
- Fashion critic
- Attorney
- Judge
- Job placement counselor
- Makeover specialist/personal stylist
- TV anchor

lawyer, or diplomat—is a natural. And with trend-setting Venus as your cosmic guardian angel, you're a natural-born fashion designer, make-up artist, and interior decorator.

Looking Good

For Libra, **personal style is all about elegance**, prettiness, and looking fashionably fab. When it comes to hair, accessories, and makeup, Libras like anything as long as it's uniquely feminine. And because you have a major obsession with coordination, everything has to match—from your underwear down to your nail polish.

Libra Fashion Passions

- Baby-soft pastel colors
- Body-skimming fabrics
- A little bit of lace (even if you're the only one who sees it)
- Anything that's one-of-a-kind
- A lucky piece of jewelry (that goes with everything, of course!)

Libra Perfect Party-Down Outfit:
Pale crocheted sweater dress with antique accessories to match

Scorpio

Chapter Eight

(October 23 to November 21)

Symbol: The Scorpion (with a truth-exposing sting)
Element: Water
Quality: Fixed (and about as firm as dry cement)
Energy: Feminine/Yin
Ruler: Pluto
Color: Maroon (and other dark, moody, and bewitching hues)
Gem: Topaz
Keywords: Magnetic, intense, self-disciplined
Flower: Chrysanthemum, geranium

Celebrity Scorpions: Hillary Clinton, Sean "Puffy" Combs, Leonardo DiCaprio, Calista Flockhart, Bill Gates, Whoopi Goldberg, Ethan Hawke, Katherine Hepburn, k. d. lang, Jason and Jeremy London, Matthew McConaughey, Demi Moore, Georgia O'Keeffe, Pablo Picasso, Prince Charles, Julia Roberts, Winona Ryder

Here Comes the Sun

Intensity is the name of the game for Scorpio. If you're born under this strong-willed sign, you take life ultraseriously. Scorpios understand the value of each and every day. And if there's something you want, you'll get it. **Nobody has more willpower, determination, and stamina than a Scorpio.**

Because Scorpio is a fixed sign, you have the exceptional ability to overcome obstacles and turn your desires into reality. Do you desperately want to make the track team? You'll wake up before dawn to run. Are you determined to fit into your sister's strapless gown for the prom? You'll force yourself to lose the weight. One warning: You have to be careful not to go overboard trying to reach your goals. If you're looking for a personal motto, **"Everything in moderation"** would be a good choice.

Scorpions can't help caring about things much more intensely than most other people. This can sometimes feel like a burden, because you don't have the ability to step back and detach yourself from the situation before making a judgment. But what Scorpio does have is an uncanny sense of knowing what's right.

Scorpion Likes:
- Figuring out the "why"
- Keeping secrets
- Helping those less fortunate
- Seeing results
- Having power

Scorpion Dislikes:
- Baring your soul
- Having scary nightmares
- Putting your life in someone else's hands
- People who aren't passionate
- Being jealous

You're exceptionally intuitive about people and events. When you've got a hunch—listen to it.

Though you like to chat and are a charming conversationalist, you almost never talk about yourself. Sure, you ask plenty of questions about other people (lots of detectives are Scorpios), but discussing your own personal life? Not likely.

Scorpio in Love

When Scorpios fall, they fall hard. No one is more **romantically intense** than a Scorpio. Like other Water signs, you can be emotional and moody, slow to commit, but very loving once you do. Scorpio passion can reveal itself in different ways—through physical attraction, jealousy, or undying devotion.

How will you know when you're truly and madly in love? When you feel comfortable enough to let your guard down and open up. Scorpios live in fear that whatever they reveal will come back to hurt them. **Any guy who wants you to trust them will have to be a good friend first**. And be tender, supportive, and true 100 percent of the time.

A love story with a Scorpio can have a storybook ending if you remember one very important thing: Don't *ever* hurt Scorpions, deceive them, or be untrue. Messing with their feelings is one thing they don't ever forgive—or forget.

Scorpio's Perfect Love Match

Scorpio's deep-flowing emotions mingle effortlessly with those of the other Water signs—**Pisces, Cancer, and other Scorps**. Pisces's selfless brand of love is the perfect match for Scorpio's "Don't Ask,

Don't Tell" badge of honor. The Water-to-Water connection also flows smoothly with Cancer. The Crab's loyal love of family helps provide the Scorpion with a sense of stability and trust. When you double up on a dose of Scorpio, romance is sure to bloom—if you can ever learn to trust each other.

The Air signs—**Aquarius, Gemini, and Libra**—tend to evaporate Scorpio's watery emotions. Aquarius's occasional spaciness can make the Scorpion lose control (and we all know what a bummer that can be). Gemini's fast-talking, aka gossipy, ways can make the Scorpion very uneasy. With Scorp's neighboring sign of Libra, the odds of a love match improve—but not a whole lot.

A Scorpio/Fire sign combo can be combustible. The spontaneous nature of the Fire signs—**Sagittarius, Aries, and Leo**—doesn't match up well with Scorpio's more deliberate tactics. Scorpio isn't impressed by honest Sag's straightforward bluntness. With the Ram, it's head-butting time as Scorpio and Aries try to prove who's the better half. The best chance for a Water/Fire connection lies with Leo. Scorpio can handle the Lion's cockiness and Leo knows how to provide Scorpion with firm, but loving, guidance. This duo shows promise—if you don't kill each other first with one-upmanship.

Scorpio's ultimate chance for a love connection lies with the Earth signs—**Capricorn, Taurus, and Virgo**. With Capricorn, the only way to take things is nice and slow, and that's a philosophy that appeals to Scorpio. Sensuous Taurus, Scorpio's opposite, is drawn to Scorpio's magnetism. Virgo's ability to uncover a secret—and keep it quiet—is a major turn-on for Scorpio. Add the Virgin's low-key attraction to the equation and you'll find that Scorpio + Virgo = a match made in heaven.

Does he rock your world or bum you out? Check out the Cosmic Love-O-Meter to find out what sign lights your fire.

Do You Sigh for Scorpions?

So you've snagged yourself a Scorpion. Here's some essential stuff you should know:

Three Ways to Get a Scorpion's Attention:

❶ Stare at him (he is way into making eye contact).
❷ Start a conversation (but don't gossip!).
❸ Be mysterious (the unknown is a major turn-on for him).

All-time Fave Scorpion Dates:

❶ Go on an adventure hike (especially if a map is involved).
❷ Watch mystery movies together (and try to figure out who did it).
❸ Just hang together, cuddling (but not if his buds are in sight).

Classic Scorpion Guy-Flicks:

1. *I Know What You Did Last Summer* (and the sequel)
2. *Cruel Intentions*
3. Any murder mystery

Classic Scorpion Guy Music:

1. Smashing Pumpkins
2. Metallica
3. Anything with Dr. Dre

You and your Scorpion have had a fight. The best ways to make up are:

1. Pull him aside and apologize (but make sure no one else is around).
2. Pass him a note written in code.
3. Keep your private life private and you'll never battle in the first place.

Super Scorpion Anniversary Gifts:

1. After one month: a list of anagrams of both your names
2. After six months: an alligator-skin diary—with a lock and key
3. After one year: a leather jacket (Scorps love animal skin.)

The Friend Factor

One thing's for sure: **Scorpios can be counted on**. When you say you're going to do something, you keep your promise, no matter what.

Nobody's got a better memory than a Scorpio. When your friend calls because she can't think of the lyrics to a song, you're the

If You're Friends with a Scorpion:

- Laugh at her jokes.
- Never compete with her for the same thing.
- Keep her private life private.
- Be generous.
- Never dis her in front of her crush.

one who's able to fill in the blanks. And you're a natural-born detective—you know the scoop on everyone. But you're no gossip. In fact you can keep your mouth zipped longer than anybody.

But Scorpio's not willing to expose her own secrets. **You'll spill your guts only when and if your friendship becomes rock-solid.** And if someone broadcasts *your* secrets—they can kiss your friendship good-bye. Eventually friends discover that you can be jealous, especially if they've got something you think you deserve more. And forget about making up. Scorps don't get mad—they get even.

School, Sports, and Work

Intellectual discovery is fascinating to a **Scorpion**—just as long as you're into the subject. Which helps explain why you can get an A+ in chemistry and an Incomplete in Spanish. Having the right teacher is important to Scorp, because if the presentation isn't stimulating, you won't allow yourself to learn. Tip to Scorpions: If you've having trouble with a class, try learning from books on tape or via the Internet. Sometimes a fresh perspective is all it takes to turn your brain's switch from Off to On.

Scorpio likes to learn by doing and would much rather perform an experiment than listen to a lecture. You're into science and math and can't get enough of any subject that satisfies your curiosity.

Due to your intense double rulers, Mars and

Typical Scorpion Careers:

- Psychiatrist
- Detective
- Medical research
- Drug counselor
- Gynecologist/ obstetrician
- Magician
- Commodities trader
- Investigative journalist

Pluto, Scorpio needs plenty of physical activity. Your body is overloaded with energy. Any activity that makes you feel in charge works best, like the martial arts or competitive biking.

When it comes time for you to figure out your life's work, only one thing really matters: **You need to see that you're accomplishing something.** Performing the same meaningless task, day after day, is not for you.

Looking Good

As the Zodiac's most passionate sign, your clothes have one purpose: to express your unique magnetism. **Intense and dramatic** are words that describe your hairstyle, makeup, and unmistakable fashion sense. Deep colors and plush fabrics totally appeal to you.

Scorpio Fashion Passions

- Fabrics that feel good to the touch (like velvet, suede, and satin)
- Lingerie
- Good-luck charms (especially if they've been in your family forever)
- Bohemian accessories
- Piercings—are there any Scorpio girls left on the planet who *don't* have pierced ears?

Scorpio Perfect Party-Down Outfit:
Leather jeans, an antique velvet camisole, and a sterling silver tribal armband

Sagittarius

Chapter Nine

(November 22 to December 21)

Symbol:	The Centaur (with dead-on aim)
Element:	Fire (all that heat keeps you revved)
Quality:	Mutable ("Que sera, sera" is cool with you.)
Energy:	Masculine/Yang
Ruler:	Jupiter (the luck-meister of the heavens)
Color:	Purple, indigo, cobalt—anything purplish-blue
Gem:	Turquoise (especially Native American pieces)
Keywords:	Honest, generous, and blunt (with a capital B)
Flower:	Carnation

Celebrity Centaurs: Christina Aguilera, Woody Allen, Tyra Banks, Kim Basinger, Ludwig van Beethoven, Emily Dickinson, Walt Disney, Darryl Hannah, Katie Holmes, JFK Jr., John Malkovich, Bette Midler, Alyssa Milano, Sinead O' Connor, Brad Pitt, Monica Seles, Frank Sinatra, Britney Spears, Steven Spielberg, Mark Twain

Here Comes the Sun

 Nobody cares more about freedom than a Sagittarius. Maybe it has to do with your half-human, half-horse symbol, the Centaur, but a Sag hates to be reined in. To the Centaur, fame, fortune, and a wardrobe of designer duds mean nothing if you're not free to do as you please.

Sag is a Mutable Fire sign. That means **you're impulsive, energetic, and an ultraquick information absorber**. It's a rare Centaur who will spend the day on the sofa watching soaps and eating ice cream out of the carton. You are a doer. Long, drawn-out lectures and in-depth intellectual discussions can drive you crazy because you can't take sitting down for any major length of time.

There's an old astrologer's proverb that says, "If you seek the truth, ask a child or a Sagittarian." The truth is, most Centaurs don't lie. It's not that you *can't* lie (you are human, after all . . . okay, *half* human). It's just that, for a Sag, telling the truth is such a natural impulse, lying never even crosses your mind.

People like Sags because they're open, forthright, and cheerful. And, unlike some of the more critical signs, Centaurs like to see the best in people. You have the rare ability to

Centaur Likes:
- Being outdoors
- Telling it like it is
- Absolute freedom
- Keeping busy
- Playing games

Centaur Dislikes:
- Liars
- Being confined
- Playing it safe
- Too much responsibility
- Negative people

accept folks for the way they are—not how you want them to be. No wonder you have such a good rep.

Sagittarius in Love

As a Sagittarius, you have to like someone before you can love them. **Friendship comes before head-over-heels infatuation.** Sure, you've got raging hormones just like everyone else, but you don't let them rule your life.

You're not subtle. If you dis someone, they'll definitely know it. You pride yourself on being honest, direct, and to the point, and expect more of the same from the object of your affections.

Anyone involved with a Sag had better be a social animal, because the Centaur loves to party. And your boyfriend had better like your buds, because he'll be seeing lots of them. Sags can be really reluctant to spend time alone with their honey.

If you're going out with a Sag, there are some things the easygoing Centaur will not accept. Lie to him, and you're history. Make promises you have no intention of keeping, and you're out the door. Want to know the absolutely fastest way to terminate this love connection? Raise your voice and demand a commitment, right this very second. The Centaur will be gone before you can even spell that dirty "C" word.

Sagittarius's Perfect Love Match

Fire-to-fire is the kind of sizzling bond that Sag just can't say no to. With **Aries**, there's never a boring moment. Both are born to party, but will Aries be able to handle the Centaur's nonstop flirting? A **Leo** and Sagittarius match rates pretty high in the love lottery, and the Centaur won't mind the Lion's nonstop need for flattery. But can Leo deal with the blunt truth? A double-**Sag** relationship has major potential because you both know what to expect from each other. But there can be such a thing as too much honesty in a relationship!

When Sagittarius meets up with the Water signs—**Pisces, Cancer, and Scorpio**—a chemical reaction occurs. You don't have to be a science whiz to know that too much water can put out a fire. With Pisces, Sag doesn't know how to handle all that touchy-feely emotional stuff, and the Fish may freak out when the Centaur speaks the (sometimes cruel) truth. House Pet Cancer's desire to stay close to home clashes with Sag's always-on-the-move philosophy. The Centaur's best H_2O merger lies with Scorpio, but only if Sag curbs the need to tell the truth, the whole truth, and nothing but the truth. Too much exposure might frighten the Scorpion away.

When Sag meets up with the Earth signs—**Capricorn, Taurus, and Virgo**—things can get kind of stressful. Taurus tends to take things nice and slow, but in the Sag book of rules, there are only two acceptable speeds: fast and zooming. A Sag-Virgin pairing? There's a definite electrical charge between you, but the line can go dead once Virgo starts to criticize. When you put Capricorn and Sag together, the odds get a little better. Though your energies are way different, you share an offbeat sense of humor. And once there's laughter, can love be far behind?

Since fire needs air to exist, it's obvious that the Centaur loves being near the Air signs—**Aquarius, Gemini, and Libra**. Aquarius shares Sag's craving for freedom and travel, so this pair can go far together. The Centaur's opposite sign of Gemini is another promising love match. You both love to gab, and everybody knows communication is key to a relationship. When Sag hooks up with Libra, passion soars. All's cool when you're one-on-one. But can Libra survive Sag's party-hearty-all-the-time mentality?

Does he rock your world or bum you out? Check out the Cosmic Love-O-Meter to find out what sign lights your fire.

Cosmic Love-♡-Meter

Sagittarius girl with:

Aries	Taurus	Gemini	Cancer	Leo	Virgo	Libra	Scorpio	Sag	Cap	Aqu	Pisces
💋	🚫	💋	🤝	💥	🚫	💋	🤝	💥	🤝	💋	🚫

 Pucker Up— Hot and Heavy Hook-Up

 Holding Hands—Born to Be Buds

 Explosive Combo— Watch Out!

 Stay Away —Or Else

Do You Crave a Centaur?

So you've snagged yourself a Centaur. Here's some essential stuff you should know:

Three Ways to Get a Centaur's Attention:

❶ Go right up to him and introduce yourself (they love friendly chicks).
❷ Participate in sports (prissy girls don't rock their world).
❸ Be blunt and truthful.

All-time Fave Centaur Dates:

❶ Play Frisbee and lounge on a blanket afterward.
❷ Travel together (exploring your own town or someplace far away).
❸ Take in a lecture (one that's light-years away from the stuff you learn at school).

Classic Centaur Guy-Flicks:

1. *South Park: Bigger, Longer, and Uncut*
2. *Point Break*
3. Any Westerns or stuff with animals in it

Classic Centaur Guy Music:

1. Fatboy Slim
2. Kid Rock
3. Britney Spears (but he'll say it's only because *you* like it)

You and your Centaur have had a fight. The best ways to make up are:

1. Apologize to him across the room in the form of sign language.
2. Send him a funny e-mail message begging his forgiveness.
3. Make up a knock-knock joke that includes your apology.

Best Centaur Anniversary Gifts:

1. After one month: a tube of sunscreen and a baseball cap monogrammed with your initials
2. After six months: hiking boots
3. After one year: horseback riding lessons

If You're Friends with a Centaur:

- Keep moving.
- Respect her rebellious side.
- Listen to her and laugh at her jokes (which is not hard to do).
- Be open-minded.
- Surround her with animals (she's critter-crazy!).

The Friend Factor

Sagittarius makes friends ultra-easily. Instead of hanging with one clique, **you have a varied roster of buds of all backgrounds**. And you're refreshingly nonjudgmental. Everyone's cool in your book, as long as they're fun to hang around with.

You're playful and adventurous, and live for

having a blast (especially if there's some kind of risk involved). Games of prediction and chance are some of your favorite activities, because you were born lucky.

If you're friends with a Centaur, just remember that they can't keep a secret because they don't understand the concept of privacy. Sags can be impatient and jittery, and that inability to sit still (or keep quiet) can drive you loco. But, hey, everybody needs to go crazy every once in a while.

School, Sports, and Work

Centaurs hate being told what to do, especially by a superauthoritative teacher. You do so much better in class when you're being taught by an easy-going instructor who can help you figure things out in your own way and on your own terms. And since antsy Sag can't sit still too long, you love subjects that allow you to get out of the classroom and into the real world.

Socializing and competing are crucial to Sag, so it's no wonder you get so psyched over sports. But you're not a sore loser and you don't need to win. Just playing the game is enough. And, as a Centaur, you love anything that has to do with horses.

Coming up with ways to earn a living shouldn't be too hard for Sag, because you're into so many things. You need a career that

Typical Centaur Careers:
- Traveling saleswoman
- Riding instructor
- College professor
- Veterinarian
- Stuntwoman
- Professional athlete
- Humanitarian
- Travel agent

combines your talk-a-thon talent with your love of travel and your natural ability to deal with the public.

Looking Good

"**B**asic" **is the keyword for Sagittarius**. When it comes to clothes, makeup, and accessories, less is definitely more. And since being able to move around is a number-one necessity for active Centaurs, constricting outfits, no matter how flattering, are out. Instead, you prefer simple day-to-day uniforms, like jeans and a T-shirt.

Sag Fashion Passions

- An all-American, casual style
- Broken-in jeans and a white T-shirt
- Either short and shaggy hair or a long ponytail or braid
- Sporty, functional jewelry
- Leather backpack (to stow your gear)

Sagittarius Perfect Party-Down Outfit:
Velvet overalls, a white tee, a dusting of bronzer and you're off!

Capricorn

Chapter Ten

(December 22 to January 19)

Symbol: The Goat (climber extraordinaire)

Element: Earth (the secret to being well grounded)

Quality: Cardinal (in charge and proud of it)

Energy: Feminine/Yin

Ruler: Saturn (the zodiac's oh-so-strict taskmaster)

Color: Black and gray (If it's subdued, it's a Cap color.)

Gem: Garnet

Keywords: Industrious, cautious, loyal

Flower: Pansies, holly

Celebrity Goats: Aaliyah, Mohammad Ali, Joan of Arc, Humphrey Bogart, Jim Carrey, Kevin Costner, Cuba Gooding, Jr., Martin Luther King, Jr., Jude Law, Jared Leto, Julia Louis-Dreyfus, Ricky Martin, Kate Moss, Elvis Presley, Diane Sawyer, Denzel Washington, Tiger Woods

Here Comes the Sun

 Like their surefooted and determined symbol, the mountain goat, **Caps *always* get to where they want to go**, no matter how rocky the climb or how long it takes to get there.

Rebellion for its own sake doesn't sit well with you. Neither does blindly going along with every trend that comes along. The Goat knows better than to jump to conclusions and react impulsively. Capricorn knows that research and reason are key to achieving results.

Goats are into organization and structure. You believe there's always a right way to do something (so what if it just so happens to be *your* way). **Hardworking and trustworthy**, you pride yourself on always being reliable, and you look down on people who don't come through for you. You're terribly status-conscious and have to plead guilty to judging a book by its cover (or judging a girl by her Hilfiger jeans).

Capricorn believes in following orders and respecting protocol. Goats never wonder why, in the twenty-first century, people still bow to queens and kings, or stop to question why you're supposed to use a certain fork and spoon for each course. Rather than question society's

Goat Likes:
- Getting things done
- Being secure
- Butt-busting work
- Following convention
- Making big bucks

Goat Dislikes:
- Being embarrassed or teased
- Not fitting in
- Wearing cheap clothes
- Loneliness
- Immaturity

customs and traditions, Caps instinctively honor and obey them. Since *somebody's* got to carry the torch, why not let Capricorn do it?

Capricorn in Love

Ever-cautious Capricorn falls in love slowly, carefully—and completely. Though you may not seem like a super-romantic (getting you to declare your love is as tough as asking your teachers to abolish report cards), once you're hooked you're affectionate and loyal. Capricorns are caring and considerate beyond belief. **This is one sign that knows how to commit.**

How do you know when a Capricorn's in love with *you*? Well, er . . . that's a tough one. It might be easier to list things a Goat *won't* do. Capricorn won't shout "I love you" from the mountaintop. **Public displays of affection just aren't in the Capricorn love manual.** And pure out-and-out flirting? Let's just say batting your eyelashes might make your Goat honey-to-be ask if you've got a problem with your contact lens.

But when the Goat finally finds someone worthy of his time, that shy exterior will give way to a mushy sweetheart who'll give you the world (but only when the world's not looking).

Capricorn's Perfect Love Match

As an Earth sign, Capricorn digs the other terra firma signs of **Taurus, Virgo, and Capricorn**. Taurus shares the Goat's passion for living large, so there'll be lots of big-time splurging. Just be sure you see more than dollar signs when you're looking into each other's eyes. A

Capricorn-Virgo hook-up can be perfection, but that bliss can turn nasty if you nit-pick each other to death. A Capricorn-to-Capricorn match-up can be heavenly in many ways, *if* you don't mind a partnership that might put business before pleasure.

When Earth meets Air, some erosion is a scientific fact. **Aquarius**, the sign that follows Capricorn, is usually too unconventional for the conservative Goat. **Gemini's** "anything-goes" attitude may drive ambitious Cap loco. And with **Libra**, the two Cardinal signs butt heads, since both want to be in-charge. Not to mention Libra having to cope with PDA-shy Capricorn.

Capricorn may enjoy the spontaneity and exuberance of the Fire signs—**Aries, Leo, and Sagittarius**—or be overwhelmed by it. Aries and Capricorn are both bossy, so lip-locking might take a backseat to arguing. Leo and the Goat are both big chatterboxes—these two will definitely have plenty to say to each other. But can the shy Goat deal with Leo's ego? When Cap and Sag make a love connection, they bring out each other's sense of humor. But they might wish they spent more time smooching and less time laughing.

Water and Earth are essential to life, right? Well, the same goes when you're talking star signs. Earthy Cap's spirit soars when the Water signs—**Pisces, Cancer, and Scorpio**—are around. Sensitive and soulful Pisces can bring out the sweetheart hidden behind the Goat's no-nonsense exterior. When Capricorn meets up with her opposite, Cancer, it's all about chemistry. Cancer just might teach Cap a thing or two about letting go—and loving it. And Capricorn's love thermometer shoots up to the triple digits when Scorpio enters the picture.

Does he rock your world or bum you out? Check out the Cosmic Love-O-Meter to find out what sign lights your fire.

Cosmic Love-♥-Meter

Capricorn girl with:

Aries	Taurus	Gemini	Cancer	Leo	Virgo	Libra	Scorpio	Sag	Cap	Aqu	Pisces
💥	💋	🚫	💋	💥	🤝	🚫	💋	💥	🤝	🚫	💋

- 💋 Pucker Up—Hot and Heavy Hook-Up
- 🤝 Holding Hands—Born to Be Buds
- 💥 Explosive Combo—Watch Out!
- 🚫 Stay Away—Or Else

Do You Get into Goats?

So you've snagged yourself a Goat. Here's some essential stuff you should know:

Three Ways to Get a Goat's Attention:

❶ Start up a conversation, but make sure what you say makes sense. (Goats are ultrapractical dudes who hate small talk.)

❷ Wear something conservative (put away that revealing outfit).

❸ Show him you're hardworking.

All-time Fave Goat Dates:

❶ People-watch at the mall.

❷ Study together—in close quarters, of course.

❸ Go to a historical museum or lecture.

Classic Goat Guy-Flicks:

- *Independence Day*
- *Citizen Kane*
- Any black-and-white classic film

Classic Goat Guy Music:

1. Matchbox Twenty
2. Will Smith
3. Any kind of big-band music

You and your Goat have had a fight. The best ways to make up are:

- Forget about it and just continue as if it never happened.
- Send him a short e-mail that says, "Sorry."
- Whatever you do, don't make a big emotional scene over it.

Best Goat Anniversary Gifts:

- After one month: a bookstore gift certificate
- After six months: anything with a designer label
- After one year: a share (or two) of stock in a prestigious company

The Friend Factor

Manners mean a lot to a Capricorn. You care about other people's feelings and keep your promises. You stick by your bud, even if she goes from head cheerleader to class burn-out at the speed of light. **If Cap was a national monument, you would be Old Faithful.**

If You're Friends with a Goat:

- Don't put her on the spot (making her sweat is a big no-no).
- Avoid peer pressure.
- Respect her opinion.
- Give her privacy.
- Help her to take life less seriously.

Making constructive use of your time is a biggie, because you hat wasting the day away. If you invite some of your buds over to listen t a hip new CD, you'll be editing a literature term paper at the same time

Okay, so you can be a bit bossy. You can also be smug about you own achievements and way too critical of others. And you're easil impressed by fame and fortune. But if your buds want a friend they ca count on, you're the one.

School, Sports, and Work

Since school is all about obeying the rules and getting ahead, it's no major surprise that the Goat is usually a great student. **You have the discipline that learning requires**, which usually results in skyscraper-high grades.

Goats tend to gravitate toward all the social sciences, shop, and home ec (you really love to follow a recipe). Most have little desire to learn a foreign language and could care less about any study that's not concrete.

Most Goats don't live for sports. But when you do work out, you like to do it solo and in the great outdoors. You also love anything that requires strategy and planning, like board games and arts and crafts.

When Capricorns choose their careers, they lean toward jobs that will help them make and keep money. Being the star doesn't interest the

Typical Goat Careers:
- Real estate agen
- Archeologist
- Financial analys
- Outward Bound leader
- Currency trader
- Systems analyst
- Politician
- Business manag

Goat half as much as pulling strings behind the scenes. **You know that the real power lies with those who manage and organize**—and not with the ones who take a bow.

Looking Good

The Goat girl would rather die than be a fashion victim! **Wearing what's considered cool is the last thing you'd do.** You much prefer one well-cut jacket from a name-brand designer to a closetful of trendy, throwaway gear. Goats usually prefer low-key hair and makeup. You may not own a ton of accessories, but the ones you do own will be the real deal.

Capricorn Fashion Passions

- Classic blue jeans
- Expensive perfume
- Real antique jewelry (especially with garnets or pearls)
- Anything vintage
- One expensive makeup item

Capricorn Perfect Party-Down Outfit:
The classic little black dress and Granny's pearls

Aquarius

Chapter Eleven

(January 20 to February 18)

Symbol: The Water Bearer
Element: Air (An air-cooled brain never overheats. It keeps going and going. . . .)
Quality: Fixed (Change my mind . . . I dare you!)
Energy: Masculine/Yang
Ruler: Uranus (the bizarro planet)
Color: Electric blue and psychedelic purple
Gem: Amethyst
Keywords: Humane, independent, experimental
Flower: Orchid, violet

Celebrity Water Bearers: Jennifer Aniston, Susan B Anthony, Brandy, Nick Carter, Sheryl Crow, Charles Dickens, Mat Dillon, Thomas Edison, Abraham Lincoln, Wolfgang Amadeus Mozart Paul Newman, Ronald Reagan, Christina Ricci, Chris Rock, Franklin D Roosevelt, Tori Spelling, Mena Suvari, Justin Timberlake, John Travolta

Here Comes the Sun

 Water Bearers are said to march to the beat of a different drummer. If the world were run only by Aquarians, bridal registries, Democrats vs. Republicans, Miss America, and naming baby boys Junior wouldn't exist. That's because you don't believe in tradition for tradition's sake. For you, shaking things up every once in a while is the only way to keep life interesting. Lots of you are activists and humanitarians. Just name the cause and Aquarius will be there, sign in hand, ready to protest. Aquarius's purpose in life? **Questioning the status quo.**

The Water Bearer brain is always full of unusual theories and ideas. You have an opinion on everything—and you're happy to share it with all who will listen (and even some who won't). Aquarians are often highly gifted in science, music, or technology. **You're on the cutting edge of *everything*.**

Independent and free-willed, Aquarius is a natural-born peacemaker. You understand that the world is filled with all sorts of people and you're open-minded enough to listen to anyone's point of view. Water Bearers don't treat folks differently depending on their social or economic status. To the Water Bearer, people

Water Bearer Likes:
- Having the freedom to be whatever you wish
- Getting your point across
- Inventing things
- Being known as an original
- Being in touch with the world

Water Bearer Dislikes:
- Having to borrow money
- Being bullied by authority
- Social injustice
- Too much emotion
- Being pigeonholed or labeled

are people, whether they're rich, poor, good-looking, or plain. You are especially drawn toward the unusual and eccentric. In fact, **Water Bearers *celebrate* diversity**. It's you who keeps the world on its toes.

Aquarius in Love

Independent Aquarius needs lots of freedom in love. **You express your feelings in a cool, calm, and detached manner.** That's not to say that Water Bearers don't get passionate. It's just that friendship definitely comes before, during, and after romance.

When you're interested in someone, they'll know it. Aquarians like lots of heart-to-hearts, and ask tons of hypothetical questions. The Water Bearer needs to be sure that: 1) The other person can be trusted, 2) He or she will tolerate any and all peculiarities, and 3) You won't be smothered.

When you're part of an Aquarian twosome, be prepared for a wild and exotic ride. While most couples are going to a blockbuster action flick, you'll be taking in a foreign or art film. While other dinner dates consist of grabbing a pepperoni slice at the mall, you two will be devouring authentic Pakistani cuisine in a remote part of town. **For Aquarius, life is one big adventure**—unconventional and sometimes bizarre, but big-time fun.

If you're going out with an Aquarian, accept the fact that you're not going to have that much time alone. Instead of just the two of you, it will be you and two—or four—buddies. And don't be possessive. Water Bearers absolutely hate jealousy and despise demands.

Aquarius's Perfect Love Match

When Aquarius meets up with the other Air signs—**Gemini, Libra, or another Water Bearer**—there's a free-floating exchange of love and ideas. With a Gemini/Aquarius hook-up, there'll be equal parts lip-locking and gabbing. The cerebral connection between Gemini and Aquarius doubles the physical attraction. When Libra is part of Aquarius's love life, the Water Bearer's softer side emerges. Look for plenty of sweet talk interspersed with discussions on how to change the world. An Aquarius-to-Aquarius coupling is like a political campaign: lots of excitement, verbal sparring, and major partying. Okay, so the romance is nothing to brag about, but, boy, can your souls connect.

When Airy Aquarius merges with the solid-as-clay Earth signs—**Taurus, Virgo, and Capricorn**—expect a dust storm. Taurus's conventional attitude doesn't sit well with free-spirited Aquarius. A Water Bearer union with prim and proper Virgo can work, but there's bound to be explosions. Putting Cap and Aquarius together is sort of like inviting your grandmother and a punk rocker to dinner: straight-up culture clash.

When you mix Air-ess Aquarius with the Water signs—**Pisces, Cancer, and Scorpio**, love often evaporates. Sensitive Pisces shares the Water Bearer's passion for helping those in need. But there's not much you'll be able to do if it's your love life that needs fixing. Close-to-home Cancer can be too rooted for free-spirited Aquarius. And the Crab's fondness for baby talk is a no-go with the Water Bearer. Superintense Scorpio is another challenging prospect for Aquarius, when you consider how tough it is for the Water Bearer to get really close to anyone on an emotional level.

Fire needs air to burn brightly, so it's only natural that the Fire signs—**Aries, Leo, or Sagittarius**—need the windblown caresses of Aquarius. With Aries, Aquarius learns how stimulating verbal combat can be. Aquarius's opposite sign of Leo radiates physical attraction. The question is, who's going to be in charge? The Water Bearer and Sagittarius share the urge to do exactly as they please. Which can explain why the only time they might see each other is when they're running out the door.

Does he rock your world or bum you out? Check out the Cosmic Love-O-Meter to find out what sign lights your fire.

Cosmic Love-♡-Meter

Aquarius girl with:

Aries	Taurus	Gemini	Cancer	Leo	Virgo	Libra	Scorpio	Sag	Cap	Aqu	Pisces
💥	🚫	💋	🚫	💥	🤝	💋	🤝	💋	🚫	💥	🤝

 Pucker Up—Hot and Heavy Hook-Up

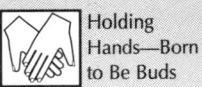 Holding Hands—Born to Be Buds

 Explosive Combo—Watch Out!

 Stay Away —Or Else

Do You Want a Water Bearer?

So you've snagged yourself a Water Bearer. Here's some essential stuff you should know:

Three Ways to Get a Water Bearer's Attention:

❶ Break the ice by saying something intriguing and bizarre.
❷ Wear a one-of-a-kind outfit (the brighter the better).
❸ Be political (he loves a girl who's involved with the planet).

All-time Fave Water Bearer Dates:

❶ Help out at a shelter or food bank.
❷ Check out obscure reading material at the bookstore.
❸ Have a romantic chat via the Internet.

Classic Water Bearer Guy-Flicks:

1. *Star Wars* (the whole series)
2. *Contact*
3. Anything animated or made independently

Classic Water Bearer Guy Music:

1. Moby
2. Jamiroquai
3. Anything techno

You and your Water Bearer have had a fight. The best ways to make up are:

1. Write him an e-mail telling him how much you miss his friendship.
2. Call him on his cell and invite him over to help you with schoolwork.
3. Ask his best bud to intervene—Aquarians respect their friends' advice.

Super Water Bearer Anniversary Gifts:

1. After one month: a new video game
2. After six months: any kind of gadget to get him stoked
3. After one year: a star named after him

The Friend Factor

Water Bearers are **supertrustworthy**. You don't talk about your buds and would never, ever spill their deepest secrets. And you don't mind putting up with their eccentricities (chances are, yours are even stranger!).

Plop a Water Bearer down anywhere in the world, and you'll have a party list full of friends before the sun sets. Because of this social ease,

If You're Friends with a Water Bearer:

- Don't expect her to conform.
- Avoid boredom.
- Feed her exotic food (she loves chopsticks).
- Follow her "Live and let live" motto.
- Surround her with lots of gadgets.

you usually have a posse of friends—young and old, black and white, straight and gay, rich and poor.

But just because you chat with loads of folks doesn't mean you get ultraclose to them. In fact, you do your best to avoid any emotional scenes. And you're spacey—forever getting caught up in your dreams, schemes, and inventions. But when you come down to earth—you know how to be a good friend.

School, Sports, and Work

Determined Water Bearers are good **concentrators**, and you always have to finish what you start. Your mad-scientist brains make you a natural at deciphering different languages, codes, or puzzles. And psychology and sociology are two of your favorite subjects because you get to delve deep into one of your favorite subjects: humankind.

Because Aquarius is so **mentally oriented**, you're usually not into disciplined exercise. But you do love being outdoors, even if it's just to swing on the hammock and read 'zines. As a Water Bearer, you should check out physical activities that take place around water.

Choosing a career is a cinch if the Water Bearer remembers one ultra-important thing: **variety**. For you, it's the only way to live. Jobs in technology are probably appealing, as are jobs that let you help people.

Typical Water Bearer Careers:
- Web page designer
- TV anchor
- Airline pilot
- Sociologist
- Electrical engineer
- Inventor
- Astronomer
- Psychiatrist
- Translator

Looking Good

Looking like the rest of the world's a drag for one-of-a-kind Aquarians. You're not afraid to break tradition and stand out in a crowd. In fact, starting trends is what you do best. Luckily, Water Bearers can get away with outfits others would never even dream of putting together. If one word summed up your personal style, it would be "**eclectic**," from your head down to your toes.

Aquarius Fashion Passions

- Well-worn jeans (hand-embroidered and patched by you, of course)
- Wild hair
- Scented oils to mix as you please
- Bold silver or platinum jewelry (you'll take modern over antique any day)
- Reversible clothing

Aquarius Perfect Party-Down Outfit:
Thigh-high skirt, authentic cowboy boots, and denim jacket.

Pisces

Chapter Twelve

(February 19 to March 20)

Symbol: The Fish (swimming with and against the current)
Element: Water
Quality: Mutable (You go with the flow of life.)
Energy: Feminine/Yin
Ruler: Neptune (the planet of inspiration and ESP)
Color: Iridescent sea green
Gem: Moonstone (February) and aquamarine (March)
Keywords: Compassionate, creative, mystical
Flower: Lotus, water lily, daisy

Celebrity Fish: Michael Caine, Chelsea Clinton, Kurt Cobain, Cindy Crawford, Billy Crystal, Erykah Badu, Drew Barrymore, James Van Der Beek, Albert Einstein, Galileo, Mia Hamm, Jennifer Love Hewitt, Spike Lee, Michaelangelo, Freddie Prinze, Jr., Elizabeth Taylor, Lili Taylor, George Washington

Here Comes the Sun

Sweet, soulful, and sensitive, Pisces can't help but get wrapped up in the world around them. Fish are benevolent and compassionate people who try to help in any situation. Your mile-high tolerance and genuine interest in others feeds your desire to make the world a better place for all of us.

Bonding with human beings and pets is a Pisces must. Easily swayed by your emotions, you can be fooled by people who aren't as nice as they appear to be. The world can sometimes seem cruel and overwhelming to the sometimes-gullible Fish.

You are generally shy, passive, and very imaginative. **Pisces are the most spiritual of the signs.** Dreamy and impressionable, you can all too easily live a life of escapism. (Pisces are especially prone to addiction. Beware of too much chocolate candy—or TV soap operas!) Like the two Pisces fish swimming in opposite directions, you sometimes have trouble figuring out what do to. But when you learn to channel your energies, your creativity is boundless.

Because Pisces is a Mutable Water sign, Fish natives are **ultra-artistic**. It's a rare Fish who doesn't paint, write poetry, or compose music. You love being surrounded by beauty in

Fish Likes:

- Pure, unadulterated romance
- Not having a schedule
- Making a difference
- Dreams, mysticism, astrology
- Being in, on, or near water

Fish Dislikes:

- Loud noise
- Being suckered (once again)
- The unfairness of life
- Tight clothes
- Alcohol and drugs

your environment. Which is why fresh flowers, scented candles, and awesome artwork are always part of a Fish's life.

Pisces in Love

Pisces craves love, romance, affection, and everything in between from a potential soul mate. **Your ideal relationship is cozy and cuddly**, with lots of hand-holding and lip-locking. You don't get caught up in the looks-only game (although you have been known to swoon over a pair of smoldering eyes). In fact, some Pisces actually prefer some minor physical imperfection.

If you're going out with a Pisces, be prepared for some **intense bonding**. This is someone who won't freak out at the idea of uttering the three sacred words you're dying to hear. And expect to watch a lot of movies with your Pisces. (This is one dude who will actually watch all those chick flicks with you!)

How can you make sure your Pisces will never, ever tire of you? Be romantic. Spend lots of time with him. And never criticize his dreams and ambitions. Your sensitive Fish needs lots of support.

Pisces's Perfect Love Match

Nothing mingles as effortlessly as a Water-to-Water connection, which is why Pisces likes being around **Cancer, Scorpio, and other Fish**. With equally sensitive Cancer, you've found somebody who really understands your moods. A Scorpio honey can be a genuine keeper because you both share a hunger for life's more sensual pleasures. When Pisces meets up with another Pisces, it can be absolute perfection. But with both Fish swimming in Dreamland, who's going to handle life's day-to-day details?

Dreamy Pisces has a mellower energy than the Air signs—**Gemini, Libra, and Aquarius**. All-action all-the-time Gemini may have a hard time dealing with Pisces's laid-back attitude. A Pisces/Libra combination seems like a lovefest at first. But underneath Libra's desire for loving lies a cool and collected person who may have trouble understanding Pisces's deep-rooted emotions. When Pisces hooks up with its neighboring sign Aquarius, the immediate outlook appears sunny and calm. But Pisces's heart could get broken by Aquarius's detached emotion.

The blaze of the Fire signs—**Aries, Leo, and Sagittarius**—can scorch Watery Pisces. Though the Fish finds the Ram physically attractive (and vice versa), a run-in with confrontational Aries can overwhelm Pisces. Romance with Leo is a mixed bag. Sure, Pisces will be mesmerized by Leo's charisma, but if the Lion starts giving the Fish advice, the attraction may fizzle out. Though Sag and Pisces share a passion for spiritual enlightenment, the Centaur's sometimes painful honesty can be too much for the Fish to handle.

The Earth signs—**Taurus, Virgo, and Capricorn**—could use a nice, cold drink of watery Pisces. The sensual Bull falls right into the Fish's dreamy way of life. There's only one problem with this perfect match: is it possible to OD on romance? When Pisces snags a Virgo cutie, these two opposite signs find each other fascinating. The Virgin just might be the one who can finally make the Fish's fantasies come true. Though practical Capricorn is worlds away from dreamy Pisces, these two lovebirds have an extraordinary chance at making love fly. Is there a nest in their future?

Does he rock your world or bum you out? Check out the Cosmic Love-O-Meter to find out what sign lights your fire.

Cosmic Love-♡-Meter

Pisces girl with:

 Pucker Up—Hot and Heavy Hook-Up

 Holding Hands—Born to Be Buds

 Explosive Combo—Watch Out!

 Stay Away —Or Else

Do You Wish for a Fish?

So you've snagged yourself a Fish. Here's some essential stuff you should know:

Three Ways to Get a Fish's Attention:

❶ Be helpful.
❷ Don't pretend to be perfect (Pisces will actually like your flaws).
❸ Don't be too aggressive (or you'll scare him away!).

All-time Fave Fish Dates:

❶ Volunteer to help the elderly or underprivileged.
❷ Hang together without saying a word (let your ESP do the work).
❸ Go to the movies (Fish love being transported to another world).

Classic Fish Guy-Flicks:

1. *William Shakespeare's Romeo and Juliet*
2. *Jaws*
3. Any film that features a dream sequence

Classic Fish Guy Music:

1. Phish (naturally)
2. Old Bob Dylan
3. Any tunes with killer lyrics

You and your Fish have had a fight. The best ways to make up are:

1. Spill your guts to him in a love letter.
2. Call him and tell him how much you miss your soul mate.
3. Leave a goodie basket—and a note—outside his house.

Super Fish Anniversary Gifts:

1. After one month: a book of poetry—dedicated to the one you love!
2. After six months: a fun-filled and romantic day at the water park
3. After one year: an aquarium filled with exotic fish

The Friend Factor

Friendship is a pretty sacred thing to a Fish. **Neither time nor distance can break the special bond you have with your buds.** Although you're not too thrilled when your friends try to give you advice, you're there to empathize and reminisce whenever *they* need *you*. And your instincts for reading people tell

If You're Friends with a Fish:

- Understand her many moods.
- Don't give her advice.
- Don't spill her secrets.
- Give her freedom to space out.
- Bring her near water.

you if you've chosen a good friend each and every time.

Dreamy Pisces can actually visualize what the future might hold. That can help you turn your goals into reality—and you're always ready to show your friends how to reach their goals, too. Since you're **totally supportive**, you're able to enjoy their successes as much as your own.

School, Sports, and Work

You know that five-year-old who was clinging to Mommy on the first day of school? That was probably a Pisces. Though leaving the comforts of the home pond was tough, once the Fish landed in school, it was smooth swimming ahead.

Pisces's natural ability to read people comes in handy for school, because you instinctively know what a teacher wants from you. This is why you so often end up at the head of the class.

It's the rare Pisces who's a jock. Sure, lots of you like to watch sports (as long as it's not violent), but working up a sweat isn't your number-one leisure activity. Getting physical in and around water is one major exception, even though you'd usually rather hang by the riverside than play around in the river.

Making money is usually not Pisces's main focus. That's why **you choose careers you love**,

Typical Fish Careers:

- Fashion photographer
- Artist
- Writer
- Psychologist
- Jewelry designer
- Research scientist
- Cruise director
- Theology professor
- Health care worker

not ones that pay the highest salaries. Since helping fellow humans makes Fish feel wanted, lots of you are in the social services and counseling professions.

Looking Good

Softness and shine are what mystical Pisces looks for in her appearance. You love to wrap your body in pastel colors and flowing, feminine fabrics. You like your accessories small and dainty. And since Fish love to be pampered, you appreciate any clothing that feels good against your skin.

Pisces Fashion Passions

- Adding feminine touches (even to plain old jeans and a T-shirt)
- Long, flowing locks
- Makeup with major shimmer
- Shoes, shoes, and more shoes
- Anything that stretches (tight clothes make you ultracranky)

Pisces Perfect Party-Down Outfit:
Angora sweater, sheer chiffon full-length skirt, and delicate ankle-strap sandals

Chapter Thirteen
Beyond Your Sun Sign

So now you know all about your Sun sign. You've learned loads about yourself—and about your friends and family. But maybe you still have the feeling you're missing something. Say you're an Aries but you aren't that bossy. Everything you read always mentions the Ram's overbearing nature, but that just doesn't describe the real you. Or say you're a Virgo—but you're really not a neatnik. Some days you need a snowplow just to get through your room. In short, your sign isn't a perfect fit. What's up?

Well, **your Sun sign is just one part of who you are**. For an in-depth look, you need to know the position of the other signs and planets when you were born, too. For that, you have to look at your natal (birth) chart.

There are a few ways to get a hold of your very own chart. You could perform intricate mathematical equations in order to figure out exactly where the planets were hanging at the precise moment of your birth. There are some great books on doing it yourself in the library or local bookstore. Or you could invest in some costly astro-software and let the computer do it for you.

You can also take the easy way out, and get a chart processed in nanoseconds. You can find a certified stargazer in the yellow pages under "Astrology." But the easiest (and cheapest) way to have a chart cast is via the Internet. Most astrological websites will do your chart for a small fee, and some of them offer their services for free. Just do a search on the Internet under "Astrology."

Let's assume you've got your natal chart in hand. It's filled with glyphs (symbols) of the planets and signs. If you look at your natal chart as a giant puzzle, you can think of each symbol as holding an important clue to a piece of that puzzle.

Besides your sun sign, the most important parts of your chart will be the rising sign and the planets.

Revealing Your Rising Sign

The sign that was rising over the horizon at the exact moment you were born is called your **ascendant or rising sign**. Your rising sign reveals the mask you wear to present yourself to the world. Sure, you might be an up-front-and-at-cha kind of Aries, but if your rising sign is Cancer, you'll be a lot less direct. The rising sign is important because it has to do with the way you present yourself—how you talk, dress, and act in front of others. Sometimes it hides your true self.

So how do you find out your rising sign? Well, because rising signs change every two hours or so, the most accurate way is to look at a bona fide chart. But if you don't have your chart in front of you, there is a way of estimating. Here's how it works.

Each morning, from approximately 6:00 a.m. to 8:00 a.m., the sign rising is the same as the Sun sign. So on the chart below, write your Sun Sign on the 6:00-8:00 a.m. line. Then fill in the signs following your Sun Sign in their correct order. Example time: If your Sun Sign is Gemini, write that on the 6:00-8:00 a.m. line. On the next line (8:00-10:00 a.m.), write in Cancer. The 10:00 a.m.-12:00 Noon line should say Leo, 12:00-2:00 p.m. Virgo, and so on. The sign that's on the line that corresponds to your time of birth is your rising sign.

Your Instant Rising Sign Decoder

12:00 Midnight–2:00 a.m. _____

2:00–4:00 a.m. _____

4:00–6:00 a.m. _____

☀ 6:00–8:00 a.m. _____

8:00–10:00 a.m. _____

10:00 a.m.–12:00 Noon _____

12:00 Noon–2:00 p.m. _____

2:00–4:00 p.m. _____

4:00–6:00 p.m. _____

6:00–8:00 p.m. _____

8:00–10:00 p.m. _____

10:00 p.m.–12:00 Midnight _____

The Planets

Everybody's chart contains all of the twelve signs and all nine planets. (In astrology, the Sun and the Moon are considered planets.) **Planets stand for different energies within ourselves.** The sign each planet is located in indicates how that planetary energy affects you.

Let's say your Sun sign is Leo. Ordinarily, you'd expect to be cheerful, outgoing, and in charge. But your ascending sign is Pisces, so the person the world sees is dreamy and somewhat shy. If your Moon is also in Pisces, you are also very sensitive and emotional. Like all Leos, you want to be a star, but you might spend more time fantasizing about success than actually achieving it.

This is what each of the planets represents:

The Sun

As the single most important planet in your chart, the **Sun symbolizes the way you approach life**. It's who you are, what you're naturally good at, and how far you'll go to get what you want. As everybody knows, the Sun takes one year to go through all twelve signs.

The Moon

Almost as important as the Sun, the **Moon indicates your emotional makeup**—your instincts, desires, hunches, feelings, and those irritating little habits that you just can't help. The Moon takes about twenty-nine days to circle the Sun.

Mercury

Tiny planet **Mercury determines your intelligence level,** mode of expression, and how you get your point across. Been called a fast-talker? Blame it on Merc. This quick-moving planet takes just eighty-eight days to make a complete spin around the solar system.

Venus

The Evening Star is the Zodiac's very own **fashion stylist**. What you wear, how you act in public, and the things (and humans) you're attracted to all fall under Venus's spell. Are you big on PDAs? That's Venus's doing. It takes 243 days for Venus to make her journey around the Sun.

Mars

Are you a weakling or a tough-gal? **Mighty Mars is the planet that**

gives you energy, courage, and physical assertiveness. In-charge Mars takes 1.88 years to do his ring around the solar system.

Jupiter

Good luck, prosperity, and the wisdom to know what to do with them all fall under Jupiter's jurisdiction. Are you superconfident or superinsecure? That's Jupiter's call. Orbiting the Sun takes Jupiter just under twelve years.

Saturn

As taskmaster of the stars, Saturn's job is to teach you some of the not-so-fun things in life, like **limits, perseverance, and discipline**. How you relate to authority figures and responsibility are also under Saturn's jurisdiction. Saturn's spin-around takes $29^{1}/_{2}$ years.

Uranus

The Age of Aquarius and all things bohemian and rowdy is what Uranus is all about. This is the planet of **independence and originality**. Because this planet takes eighty-four long years to circle the Sun, the sign Uranus is in is considered generational.

Neptune

Dreams, ESP, hunches, spirituality, and illusions are all part of Neptune's dominion. Another slow-orbiter generational planet, Neptune takes 165 years to make its way round the Sun.

Pluto

Intense Pluto is the heavy of the astro-world. **Transformation, rebirth, and the unconscious** are a few of the powerful realms handled by our faraway, but oh-so-powerful, planet. Talk about taking your time, Pluto needs 248 years to make his way around the Sun.

What a Chart Looks Like

How does all this astro-wisdom come together? Let's look at a sample chart to find out. Katie Holmes's chart appears on the following page.

This chart is what we call a solar chart, as opposed to a natal chart. Because we don't have the exact time of Katie Holmes's birth, this chart does not include the rising sign or other information. But there's still lots we can learn from just the Sun sign and the planets.

First, you might want to look at the symbol chart on page 3, so you can remind yourself what the symbols mean. Since Katie's a Sagittarius, you can see there's quite a few of that sign's symbol, which looks kind of like a bow and arrow. Her Sun ☉, Mercury ☿, and Neptune ♆ are in Sag ♐, which means she's a typical Centaur—honest, direct, and completely free of bull. Since the Sun represents how you approach life, **Katie's Sun in Sag means she goes after things in an honest, direct, and adventurous way**. Mercury is the planet that determines how you think and talk. Katie's is in the what-you-see-is-what-you-get sign of Sag, so her brain works in a straightforward manner. But it also shows she's got a killer sense of humor and is truly talented in mimicry (perfect for an actress, huh?). With Neptune, the planet of dreams and illusion, in Sag, Katie's most definitely an optimist.

Over on the other side of her chart, near the 2 o'clock position, you can see there are two planets in the sign of Leo ♌—the Moon ☾ and Jupiter ♃. With the Moon (the planet of how you feel) in Leo, Katie's emotional makeup is very much like a Lion—she's **passionate, determined, and full of pride**. Jupiter (the planet of luck and ambition) is also in grandiose Leo, so we can assume she's generous, enthusiastic, and theatrical.

Let's look at the love planets, Venus ♀ and Mars ♂. Venus is up toward the top of her chart, at the 11 o'clock position, and it's in Scorpio ♏.

Katie Holmes's Solar Chart

Born: December 18, 1978
Location: Toledo, Ohio

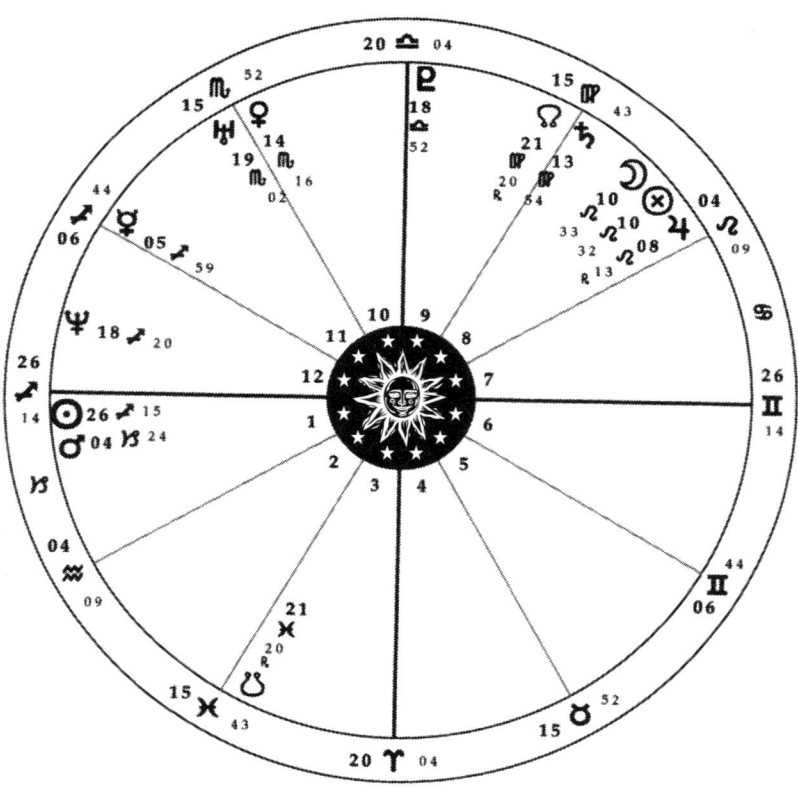

Prepared by:
Georgia Routsis Savas

Mars is just below the Sun to the far left of the chart (in the 9 o'clock spot) and it's in the sign of Capricorn ♑.

Venus is the planet that shows how you express affection. Venus in the emotional but mega-private sign of Scorpio means that Katie loves deeply and is probably more than a bit possessive of her beaus. Mars, on the other hand, describes strength and aggression. Since Mars is in the determined and practical Capricorn, Katie is definitely aggressive in going after what she wants and has a hard time with rejection.

That's a quick summary of the signs a few of her major planets are in. But let's look a little deeper into her chart and check out the connections some of the planets have with each other.

There are two knock-out planet connections in Katie's chart. The first is the Sun/Mars conjunction. (When two planets occupy the same space, that's called a conjunction.) As you can see (in the 9 o'clock spot on the chart), these two planets are almost on top of each other. This conjunction makes a person restless, competitive, and determined—with a boiling hot temper.

The other major key point in Katie's chart is her Moon/Jupiter conjunction in the 2 o'clock spot. This combo tells the story of **somebody with a wild sense of humor who thinks and feels truly, madly, and deeply**.

What's the total astro picture for Katie? Well, if you look back at the last few paragraphs, the same words keep cropping up: emotional, deep, determined. So even though Katie Holmes appears to be sweet, shy, and laid-back, **this is a girl who's got super-intense feelings—and who is not afraid to go after her goals**. Sounds like a winning combo for a successful actress, don't you think?

So now you know all about what a Sun sign means and you've seen a sample chart. This isn't all there is to know about astrology—not by a long shot. If you're still hungry for more, more, more, check out your local library or bookstore for some additional learning materials. Or do a search on the Internet. There are tons of great websites that can help steer you in the right direction.

Now that you have the 411 on astrology, let's turn to two other cool subjects that can also tell you about yourself: Chinese astrology and numerology.

Chinese Astrology

Like Western astrology, Chinese astrology tries to make sense of things. But forget about Suns and Moons—**in the Chinese version of astrology, it's all about animals**. According to legend, Buddha threw a party and invited the entire animal kingdom to attend, but only twelve animals showed up. To reward them, Buddha gave each one his or her own year. So, every twelve years, the cycle of animals repeats: Rat, Ox, Tiger, Rabbit, Dragon, Snake, Horse, Sheep, Monkey, Rooster, Dog, Boar. You share the characteristics of the animal that's listed for the year you were born.

Chinese astrology works on a lunar calendar, which is based on the number of times the Moon revolves around the Earth (unlike the Western solar calendar, which relies on the orbit of the Earth around the Sun). So each animal year starts with the New Moon of late January or early February.

Animal Attributes

The Year of the Rat
(Feb. 15, 1972–Feb. 2, 1973 / Feb. 2, 1984–Feb. 19, 1985 / Feb. 19, 1996–Feb. 7, 1997):

Rats are charming Honest Abes and are into gossip and the tabloids.

They love bargains and anything secretive and have been known to pick fights.

The Year of the Ox

(Feb. 3, 1973–Jan. 22, 1974 / Feb 20, 1985–Feb. 8, 1986 / Feb. 8, 1997–Jan. 27, 1998):

As an Ox, you're gentle yet strong and there's no bull about you—you call them as you see them. You love home cooking and can be kind of a lazybones.

The Year of the Tiger

(Jan. 23, 1974–Feb. 10, 1975 / Feb. 9, 1986–Jan. 28, 1987 / Jan. 28, 1998–Feb. 5, 1999):

Tigers are free with their cash and like to be appreciated. They'll gladly accept your compliments. But just try to boss them around!

The Year of the Rabbit

(Feb. 11, 1975–Jan. 30, 1976 / Jan. 29, 1987–Feb. 16, 1988 / Feb. 6, 1999–Feb. 4, 2000):

Sensitive and refined Rabbits are obedient creatures. But underneath that shy exterior, Bunnies are blessed with a gut-busting sense of humor.

The Year of the Dragon

(Jan. 31, 1976–Feb. 17, 1977 / Feb. 17, 1988–Feb. 5, 1989 / Feb. 6, 2000–Jan. 23, 2001):

Flame-breathers are dynamic and simply irresistible. They dread boredom and hate being on a schedule. And they'll never admit they're wrong.

The Year of the Snake

(Feb. 18, 1977–Feb. 6, 1978 / Feb. 6, 1989–Jan. 26, 1990 / Jan. 24, 2001–Feb. 11, 2002):

Sophisticated and perceptive Snakes know how to impress—and love the applause. But they're also big believers in revenge, so watch your step!

The Year of the Horse

(Feb. 7, 1978–Jan. 27, 1979 / Jan. 27, 1990–Feb. 14, 1991 / Feb. 12, 2002–Jan. 31, 2003):

These bucking broncos are energetic, enthusiastic, and ever-cheerful. So what if they're always late and spend money like a counterfeiter?

The Year of the Sheep

(Jan. 28, 1979–Feb. 15, 1980 / Feb. 15, 1991–Feb. 3, 1992 / Feb. 1, 2003–Jan. 21, 2004):

Being the center of attention comes naturally to the Sheep. She's artistic and creative, but can't handle any heavy-duty emotional scenes.

The Year of the Monkey

(Feb. 16, 1980–Feb. 4, 1981 / Feb. 4, 1992–Jan. 22, 1993 / Jan. 22, 2004–Feb. 8, 2005):

Quick-witted Monkeys love to break the rules. They live for parties and games. But take away their cash and all that's left is big-time insecurity.

The Year of the Rooster

(Feb. 5, 1981–Jan. 24, 1982 / Jan. 23, 1993–Feb. 9, 1994 / Feb. 9, 2005–Jan. 28, 2006):

Attention and flattery will get you everywhere with the Rooster. But watch her cock-a-doodle-doo when anybody tries to pry into her private life.

The Year of the Dog

(Jan. 25, 1982–Feb. 12, 1983 / Feb. 10, 1994–Jan. 30, 1995 / Jan. 29, 2006–Feb. 17, 2007):

Loyal and affectionate, Dogs crave companionship. Their standards are sky-high. Adhere to them or they'll criticize you faster than you can say, "Woof"!

The Year of the Boar

(Feb. 13, 1983–Feb. 1, 1984 / Jan. 31, 1995–Feb. 18, 1996 / Feb. 18, 2007–Feb. 6, 2008):

These easygoing oinkers are generous, inventive, and easy to forgive. Now if they could only stop themselves from believing everything they hear.

Numerology – What's Your Number?

Numbers play a big part in most people's lives. Just about everybody's got a lucky number. And, somehow, those numbers keep popping up over and over. Numbers are so **powerful** that lots of folks choose a place to live by the number of the address. Athletes wear their lucky number on their backs. But not all numbers are thought of as lucky: Think about how superstitious the world is about the number thirteen. Most high-rise buildings don't even have a thirteenth floor!

The **ancient science of studying numbers is called Numerology**. Like astrology, it's another supercool way to gain insight into who you are. The ancient Greek philosopher Pythagoras is credited with coming up with this number-based science. Those early scientists believed that the mysteries of the universe could be deciphered by the numbers 1 through 9. And they found that each of these numbers resonates to a specific cosmic vibration. **These numbers play a major part in determining who you are and what part you can play in the world.**

The really fab thing with numerology is how split-second easy it is to get into. Forget about knowing the exact time of your birth and sending away for your chart. With numerology, all you have to know is the birth date and full name of the person (including their middle name) you want to analyze and presto! Instant reading.

Chart of Numbers

1	2	3	4	5	6	7	8	9
A	B	C	D	E	F	G	H	I
J	K	L	M	N	O	P	Q	R
S	T	U	V	W	X	Y	Z	

It's amazingly basic: Each letter of the alphabet corresponds to a number. The letter "G" is a "7," and "S" is a "1."

Let's use a practice name to get comfy. Let's try one of the coolest—and most versatile—actresses around—Reese Witherspoon.

R E E S E   W I T H E R S P O O N

9 5 5 1 5   5 9 2 8 5 9 1 7 6 6 5

  9+5+5+1+5   5+9+2+8+5+9+1+7+6+6+5

      25   63

   2+5=7   6+3=9

    7   +   9   = 16

    1   +   6   = 7

When you add up all the numbers in a name, that's your destiny number. Reese's number is 7. What does a destiny number mean? It describes what you've been put on planet Earth to accomplish. Kind of like your very own personal mission this time around.

In numerology, every complex number gets reduced down to a single number, except when the total is 11 or 22. Those two numbers are considered master numbers because they vibrate to a higher level. In other words, if you're an 11 or 22, you're gifted.

Now, the moment you've been waiting for. Let's find out your destiny number.

First, write out your full name. Write down the numbers that correspond to each letter in your name and add them all together. When you reduce that number down to a single digit (unless, of course, the number's an 11 or 22), you'll arrive at a destiny number you can call your own.

The 411 On Destiny Numbers

If You're a One

Ones know how to go it alone. You're determined, principled, and 100 percent original. I guarantee that at some point in your life, you've been called opinionated and bossy. Guess that's why you're number one!

If You're a Two

Twos are sensitive, supportive, and great listeners. Peace and love are crucial to Twos. Keep listening to those right-on hunches, because you've got instinct and maybe even ESP.

If You're a Three

Threes are the comedians of the bunch. You're creative, flirtatious, and dramatic. So what if you get carried away with storytelling? You have to express yourself or you'll burst!

If You're a Four

If there's a war or riot, everybody runs to a Four. You're **hardworking, practical, and ultraloyal**—qualities that keep the world spinning when everybody else is lounging around by the pool. Keep up the good work!

If You're a Five

Adventure Girl could be your code name. Always on the go, **Fives are flexible, charismatic, and have trouble finishing things.** Being tied down and having to conform to outdated traditions make you freak!

If You're a Six

Like a Girl Scout, Sixes promise to protect family and country. **Responsibility is your middle name**, and there's nothing you like more than to be of service. You're into cooking and love (not necessarily in that order)!

If You're a Seven

Chaos makes introspective and solace-seeking Sevens go ballistic. **You're analytical, intellectual, and kind of eccentric.** Though you appear shy, you're really observing and absorbing every single thing that goes on around you.

If You're an Eight

Eights get off on Power. You've got **ambition, drive, and talent** to spare. Lots of things come easily to you, including decision-making and amassing piles of cold, hard cash.

If You're a Nine

If anybody's ever going to bring the world together, it'll be a Nine. Your natural peacemaking abilities can really make an impact wherever you go. **Dynamic, sensitive, and poetic**, you can be a guru—or a cult leader.

If You're an Eleven

You're here to change people's lives, whether you like it or not. **Elevens are intuitive, spiritual, and artistic**, and they are constantly revving their engines with nervous energy. This is the sign of fame and fanatics, so take your pick.

If You're a Twenty-two

If anybody's gonna make a difference around here, it's Twenty-two. You're powerful and visionary and are lucky enough to see the whole picture without getting bogged down in the details. Get going!

Astrology in Your Future

So now you've got the lowdown on astrology, Chinese astrology, and numerology. But those three faves are just the beginning! If you want more, there's a whole world of astrology waiting to be explored. In this book we've concentrated on natal astrology—how your birth chart can help you understand yourself. There's also career astrology, relationship astrology, and predictive astrology (otherwise known as horoscopes), and a lot more. Astrology can reveal the secret of you—and help you on your path through life. Happy journey!

Free gift from Neutrogena

To get a great deal on a subscription to **seventeen** magazine and a FREE gift from Neutrogena, log on to www.enews.com/seventeenbook. Or call **800-388-1749** and mention code 5BKA7

seventeen BOOKS... FOR THE TIMES OF YOUR LIFE

0-06-440871-X

How to Be Gorgeous
The Ultimate Beauty Guide to Makeup, Hair, and More
By Elizabeth Brous, beauty director of **seventeen**

Seventeen's guide to looking glam includes:
- Awesome makeup tips
- Secrets for healthy, gorgeous skin and hair
- Ways to find the best look for you— without spending a fortune
- And much, much more!

Don't delay! It's your turn to be gorgeous!

The Boyfriend Clinic
The Final Word on Flirting, Dating, Guys, and Love
By Melanie Mannarino, senior editor of **seventeen**

Do you have questions about love and relationships? Relax—**seventeen**'s got you covered. With answers to such questions as:
- How do I get a boyfriend?
- Is he the right guy for me?
- How do I know it's really love?

It's your love guide—now put it to work!

0-06-447235-3

Available wherever books are sold.

Books created and produced by Parachute Publishing, L.L.C., distributed by HarperCollins Children's Books, a division of HarperCollins Publishers.
© 2000 PRIMEDIA Magazines, Inc., publisher of **seventeen**. **Seventeen** is a registered trademark of PRIMEDIA Magazines Finance Inc.

AN EXCITING FICTION SERIES FROM *Seventeen*

LOOK FOR A NEW TITLE EVERY MONTH!

They're ready for life. They're ready for love. They're *Turning Seventeen*.

Follow four high-school heroines—Kerri, Jessica, Erin, and Maya—during the most exciting time of their lives. There's love, friendship, and huge life decisions ahead. It's all about to happen—just as they're *Turning Seventeen*.

Turning Seventeen #1
Any Guy You Want
By Rosalind Noonan
0-06-447237-X

Turning Seventeen #2
More Than This
By Wendy Corsi Staub
0-06-447238-8

Turning Seventeen #3
For Real
By Christa Roberts
0-06-447239-6

Turning Seventeen #4
Show Me Love
By Elizabeth Craft
0-06-447240-X

Available wherever books are sold.

Books created and produced by Parachute Publishing, L.L.C., distributed by HarperCollins Children's Books, a division of HarperCollins Publishers.
©2000 PRIMEDIA Magazines, Inc., publisher of **seventeen**. **Seventeen** is a registered trademark of PRIMEDIA Magazines Finance Inc.